Trials of the Working Parent

The Busy Mom's Guide to Kids, Work & Loving Yourself

K.C. Dreisbach, LMFT

For information or questions with regard to this book or the author, please contact krystal.dreisbach@gmail.com.

ISBN: 9781094901084

Thank You for Reading!

Enjoy your FREE ebook!

Thank you for your interest. I appreciate you so much that I would like to offer you a **FREE** ebook edition of my book, *Eliminating Temper Tantrums: 4 Keys to Mastering Your Child's Anger Outbursts.*

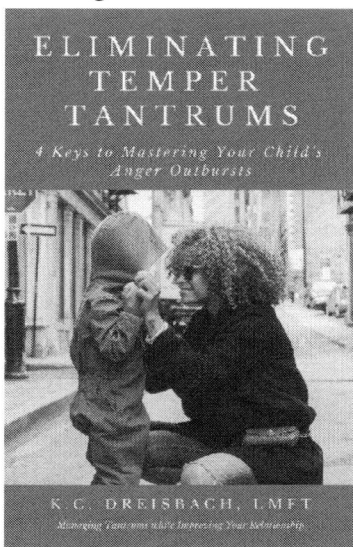

Simply visit
www.kcdreisbach.com/gift-free-ebook
to claim your FREE book.

DEDICATION

This book is dedicated to my daughter, Rachel, who is, and always will be, one of my greatest inspirations and joys in life. I love you my Angel.

CONTENTS

1. AN INTRODUCTION

Aren't you just tired of feeling like you are always working? As if there is no end to your day, just work, work, work? Don't you ever think to yourself that there has got to be a better way to manage your time, day, and life?

As a working mom, I quickly came to realize that raising kids wasn't going to be easy, especially while juggling my career. After desperately trying to find the answers to my parenting struggles in online blogs and popular baby books, I soon came to understand that the "right" book wasn't out there for me, because it didn't exist!

In this day and age, the era of the stay-at-home mom is slowly starting to die, while the reality of the working mom is quickly becoming the standard. The hard truth is, however, that the world continues to cater to the family that can afford to have one parent in the home to raise their kids! That means that there is little, if any, solutions offered to a household of working parents.

What if I was to tell you that there is a book written just for you, the parent who works all day long, and then comes home only to work all evening in caring for your home and family? What if I was to tell you that your home-life doesn't have to feel so chaotic and out of control? What if I were to tell you that one book could help you regain some balance between your family and your career?

Trials of the Working Parent has been designed to give you the answers to some of those questions that have been burning in your mind with no solutions! It was designed and written especially for the busy parent; the parent who can barely find time to shower, let alone, read a book! *Trials…* was written for YOU!

As a mother of two children under the age of 5, and as a licensed Marriage and Family Therapist with over 7 years of professional experience in working with children and families, I've brought together research and real-life examples to give you a book with the answers you've been looking for.

Like you, I was caught in the rat-race at work, slaving away in my career in order to climb up the corporate ladder, while at home, I was burning the midnight oil trying to find time to care for my family and household. I lacked balance… I lacked fulfillment… I lacked sleep! And I couldn't find the answers anywhere, but I knew that something had to change. I had to find a new way of tackling the different aspects of my life, or I was going to totally and completely burn out!

Eventually, I discovered I had the answers sitting right in front of me! I had all the tips, tricks, and ideas to make my life so much better, right at my fingertips. That's when I decided that I needed to share them with other parents just like me!

After interviewing hundreds of families who were successfully managing the work-life balance, I knew that their secrets and wisdom needed to be shared with the world, creating the very first book to tackle the reality of all working parents out there today!

Trials of the Working Parent is a unique, easy-to-read book, jam-packed with tested tips from families of all walks of life. Whether you are a single parent, stay-at-home-mom, or working parent, these tips will help you manage your life and achieve greater balance, helping you to feel more accomplished and less burned out. From tips on discipline and sleep-training, to great ideas on how to save time with household chores, *Trials…* will provide you with new concepts to help you tackle many of your parenting struggles.

Aren't you tired of going to sleep at night feeling like you got nothing done? Aren't you fed up with feeling as though your life is nothing but work? Aren't you tired of always feeling guilty because you're not spending more time with your kids? No parent should have to go through life feeling this way! So why should you?

Throughout the course of the next few chapters, you will read tips and tricks proven to successfully help busy parents find a balance between their home-life and their jobs. Each chapter will provide you with the real-life experiences of working parents who have managed to successfully make it all work, as well as research to help you decipher the myths from the truth. Finally, by the end, you will have developed new insight into yourself, helping you to shove away the guilt-ridden feelings that so many working parents face but so few are willing to talk about.

It's time to take control and no longer feel overwhelmed by your day to day existence. It's time to discover a life of balance, a life of joy, and a life of fulfillment. It's time to learn about the *real* trials of the working parent and solve them for good!

Getting Started

I believe that the best lessons are learned from life itself, from the everyday experiences of trying hard and doing your best. As such, I thought it would be important to talk to as many working moms and dads that I possibly could. I interviewed many working parents and complied all of that information to create this very book. Their combined experiences and advice, along with clinical research is what is presented here. My hope is that you will laugh, feel understood and validated, and feel inspired enough with some new ideas to tackle the rest of your child's developing years.

Next, you will find that I discuss many different topics throughout this book, and that not all of these topics will be relevant to you. Feel free to skip around and only read the chapters that spark your interest. There is no need to read the book from cover to cover. So skim through, read what seems to be relevant to you and your current stage, and ignore the rest.

With that said, let me make a few final notes. Child-rearing is a very controversial topic, and people have a tendency of becoming very offended when recommendations are made on how to raise their kids. This is especially true if the recommendations do not match their personal parenting philosophy. As such, I want to make sure we start off on the right foot. The ideas presented in this text are exactly that… ideas! They are suggestions, tips, and tricks. I believe every single family is different, and what works for one does not always work for the other. That is the reason why any given parenting technique out there today does not always work for everybody. I can also say that every child is completely different as well, regardless of the fact that they have the same parents, same environment, or same DNA. This is a FACT. So just like parenting techniques do not always work for every family, they also don't work for every child in a family.

Next, this book is not intended to be a "one stop shop." Although I tried to cover as many topics as I could, you will find that there might not be enough detail on something, or perhaps I did not cover a specific topic you were hoping for. My idea for this book was for it to be a companion to your favorite parenting style or child-rearing text. So please, do look around at other baby/toddler books out there, and then feel free to use the tips and suggestions here alongside your chosen child-rearing text.

Finally, you might catch me saying "he" as

representing both male and female. This is just for the sake of making this book easier to write and read. I mean no offense. Furthermore, I do my best to refer to child-rearing in gender-neutral ways (i.e. parenthood), but I'm sure, from time to time, I might say "motherhood" or "being a mom" etc. This is not intended to ignore the great dads out there raising their own families, and this book is just as much for them as it is for the mamas. I also may reference a "spouse" or a "partner." This is not to exclude the amazing single-parents out there. So please, accept my apologies now and think no more of it as we continue forward.

With that said, I wish you luck on your journey of parenthood, and I hope that my own story gives you great inspiration for the rocky, but joyous, road to come! Good luck!

2. GOING BACK TO WORK

The Emotional Struggle of Guilt
vs
The Satisfaction of a Career

It would only make sense to go straight to the point and discuss the obvious: going back to work. Everything else in this text is going to revolve around this central point. Going back to work is a double-edged sword without a doubt. There are parents out there who are happy to be back in the workforce and don't look back. The reality is, however, that most parents struggle with guilt when going back. This guilt exists on two levels usually:

1. You feel guilty because you left your baby or toddler at daycare and you feel you should be with them.

2. You feel guilty because you kind of like doing

something non-baby related, which means you feel terrible because you're admitting you actually like not being around your baby.

When I had Rachel, I was completing an internship that was required for my Master's program, and I was also finishing up my last quarter of classes. I had two weeks off after Rachel was born, and then, I had to go back to school. My internship allowed me to have the full, six weeks off for maternity leave, so it wasn't too bad. My husband, David, had just started a new job a few months before, so he wasn't able to use the Family Medical Leave Act (FMLA) to take time off of work to watch the baby. Where I had some luck was that my mother was self-employed as a tax accountant, and she was able to come in and live with us for two weeks to watch the baby while Dave worked and I went back to school.

I remember getting into my car that first day and looking through the window of my house, watching my mom rock my baby in her arms. And I remember crying the whole 30 minute drive to school because I was tired, sore, and wanted nothing else than to cuddle with my baby. I was bitter and angry that I could not stay behind and bond with Rachel. This was guilt number 1, the Guilt of Abandonment. I felt like a horrible mother leaving Rachel behind in the arms of someone who was *not* her mother or father. Though I was leaving her with her grandmother, I still felt awful! This is where I tip my hat to the parents who have to do this part with strangers. I can only imagine how much more of a wreck I would have been if I had to leave Rachel for the first time at a daycare with someone I hardly knew! To all the mamas and papas out there that manage this one, I salute you....

I did not feel guilt number 2 until I went back to work after maternity leave. At this point, I was sleep deprived, stressed out at school, frustrated with life, and felt totally inept at raising a baby. By this time, my mother had gone back to work. We would drop the baby with my dad while Dave and I worked. Guilt number 2 struck me when I sat at my desk in my office diligently working through my tasks. Even though the day was busy, I remember *liking it!* I liked it because I was getting to have adult conversations without the interruption of an infant's cry. I liked it because I could eat my boring sandwich at lunch all in one sitting, without needing to cradle a baby at the same time! One of the best parts of being at work was the silence; just the silent hum of the computer and nothing else. Then, I felt guilty... How could I possibly enjoy being away from my baby? Was I a terrible mother? This is the Guilt of Freedom.

All I ever remember reading on blogs and in books was about how wonderful it is to have your child: the bonding is fantastic, breastfeeding is a gift, napping with your baby is a joy, etc. And, although I do believe a lot of people feel this way about any *one* given aspect of child-rearing, I find it hard to believe that *everyone* enjoys *every* single part of it *all* the time. I remember one of my girlfriends telling me that if she had been a stay-at-home-mom, she might have killed her oldest daughter. Now, I know she was joking, but I totally get what she meant. When you combine sleep deprivation, household chores, the regular stresses of life, and have a kid who is particularly needy or stubborn, then, yeah, going to work feels like a vacation!

The important part to remember is that your child is going to be *ok* and you are *not* a bad parent. Did you get that? Your baby will grow up just fine, well adjusted, and so on and so forth. You are also a good parent! Enjoying your job does not mean you are a bad parent. It means exactly what I just said; you enjoy your work. You are probably very good at what you do and you probably have fantastic work-ethic. If you want, think of it this way, you are modeling for your child the value of hard work and doing your work well. This is something he or she will need in the future for school and for their chosen future profession. You are also modeling dedication, commitment, drive, and motivation. Again, all things that will help your child excel in school and in life! Remember, we are our children's first teacher, and what we teach them is what will shape them into who they become. Have you ever said a curse word in front of your kid and they then repeat it back to you? Or have you ever done something, like pacing while talking on the phone, and then noticed your child was doing the exact same thing with a play phone? This is what I am talking about... **modeling**. If you model motivation, then your children will begin to mirror motivation right back to you.

The guilt is normal and it is part of being a parent who has to work. You are allowed to feel crummy, you are allowed to feel bitter and angry, and you are allowed to secretly enjoy a break from your baby. No one will judge you for this... I certainly do not.

A Job... Because You "Need the Money"

Sometimes we go back to work, not because we *want* to or because our job is awesome and we *live* for our careers, but because we don't have a choice. This was the case with one of my girlfriends. Lots of people fantasize about being the stay-at-home-parent and imagine joining play groups and home schooling their kids, but sometimes these dreams are just not possible. My one girlfriend was pregnant with her first baby boy, and she wanted nothing else than to be a stay-at-home-mom. I remember when we were kids playing with Barbie dolls, she would always leave the biggest room of her dollhouse for the nursery. In fact, Barbie didn't even have a bed, just the baby. My girlfriend worked very hard to have this baby, trying for many years before realizing she and her husband were going to need infertility treatments. Once her son's due date was around the corner, she began fighting tooth and nail to stay home. The sad reality, however, was that it was not an option. It was not an option because they needed the money.

Going back to work because you "need the money" is the unfortunate reality for many working parents. Having a spouse who can stay at home is truly a luxury in many cases, especially in certain states like California, where the cost of living is just too expensive. In these situations, the Guilt of Abandonment triumphs usually, and you feel horrible because other people are spending more time with your kid than you are. One of my other girlfriends often works with children in play therapy. One day she said to me, *"I spend more time playing with other people's kids than I do with my own son, and that just seems wrong to me."*

Just as I mentioned, you are not a bad parent because you have to work. It sucks, and you are allowed to hate it and curse all the way to the office, but it is not your fault. More importantly, your child will be just fine! Just as before, every time you go to work when you don't want to, you are modeling positive things to your children, such as perseverance, commitment to your family, and motivation. These are all things that will serve your child well in the future. I remember as a child telling my dad that I didn't want to go to school. He replied, *"I don't want to go to work either, but it's important and we have to."* When you go to work to fulfill your financial obligations, regardless of what you really want to do (like stay home), you are teaching your child responsibility.

So, give yourself a break, and the next time you feel guilty about going to work, coach yourself through it and remind yourself that you are teaching your child important life lessons.

3. CAREGIVERS, BABYSITTERS & DAYCARES… OH MY!

So, you have decided, for whatever the reason, that you need to go back to work. The next big thing is to decide where your baby is going while you work. Some companies offer childcare on-site. This is great because, if you are lucky, you can check in on your babe throughout the day. (Yay for that!) But a lot of places do not offer this. So what are your next options?

I have to admit that I was very lucky. Rachel was able to stay with my parents during the day while David and I worked. My mom worked from home and my dad was retired. I was fortunate because I did not face many of the same childcare issues that many parents have to deal with.

Here is how I see it, childcare options boil down to three main possibilities:

1. Caregivers

2. Daycares

3. Babysitters

I define a *Caregiver* as someone you know and trust to care for your child in your absence. In my situation, I had caregivers. I define *Daycares* as a place where a bunch of kiddos go to be watched by licensed and certified instructors. Most places like KinderCare and Montessori Schools fall into this category. Finally, I define a *Babysitter* (or *Nanny*) as a person whom you do not know that you hire to watch your kids at home. These individuals may or may not be licensed and certified to do so. These people range from individuals hired from a professional service to high school kids needing some extra change in their pockets. There might be a few more options out there, but I believe it pretty much comes down to these three.

Working parents have to face the reality that, at some point, they will need to leave their children in the care of someone else, and this is a depressing, frustrating, and (sometimes) guilt-ridden thing to do. This predicament is made much worse if you are the parent of a child with special needs. (I tip my hat to you every day.) So, how do you go about choosing one of these possibilities? Picking one of these options will completely depend on your financial situation, available support from family and friends, and what is actually available to you in your area.

Eventually, I decided to put Rachel into a daycare because I believed she needed the socialization with other kids, but it was a hard decision to make… and an expensive one too. David and I started putting money aside for daycare approximately six months before she started attending, and I remember thinking to myself that rice, beans, and potatoes was going to be dinner for the next several months so that we could accommodate the extra cost. I also vividly remember the day I reserved her spot at the daycare about five months before her starting date. I remember looking at all the babies and toddlers running around and then sobbing like an idiot. The employees there were very sweet and told me she would be fine, encouraging me to call to check in on her. They did not realize I was just putting a deposit down! They thought I had just dropped her off for the first time. When I admitted to them that Rachel was not going to be starting for another five months, one of them laughed. I wasn't offended… I would laugh at me too! The point is that going back to work is hard, and sometimes you have no choice. There are some suggestions, however, that I can make to help this process become a little easier for you.

Daycares

First off, be informed about where your child is going. If you are placing them in a daycare or preschool, please research the place first before signing them up. Check out reviews online or ask your co-workers where their kids are going and how they like it. Be sure to go visit the facility too. In fact, I highly recommend doing several "drive bys" without having an appointment. This will allow you to see how accommodating the staff is when you catch them by surprise and how they react under stress/pressure. You will get to see how things really are when they have no idea you are coming. Do note, however, that some really places are by appointment only. In such a case, just follow the rules and make appointments as requested, but please still visit several times.

When visiting these places, there are several things you should look for. To begin, is the facility clean? Now, many daycares are located in old buildings. Just because the place is "old" or "rundown" does not mean that it is not *clean*. Smell the air, look at the floors, check the tables and chairs, etc. Does it smell like urine all the time? Are there puddles on tile floors that are not being attended to? Are the bathrooms clean? Are they making sure the kids wash their hands? How are food and drinks stored? Is it safe? Any exposed wiring or outlets that are not covered up? Do the tables have sharp corners that are not padded? These questions are just some examples of things you might want to ask about and take a look at when you visit.

Next, you might want to find out what the child-to-staff ratio is, especially if you have an infant you are placing in the daycare. The child-to-staff ratio is basically how many children there are to every one adult staff member. The daycare I put Rachel in had a 6 to 1 child-to-staff ratio, meaning that there were six children for every one adult.

Many daycares have different "rooms." There are usually an Infant Room, Toddler Room, and Preschool Room. They might have different names like Caterpillar Room or Butterfly Room, but it pretty much breaks down to Infant/Baby Rooms (roughly ages 1 month to about 2 years), Toddler Rooms (2 years to about 4 years), and Preschool Rooms (4 years to about 5 years). With that said, each of these rooms might have a different child-to-staff ratio. For example, Rachel's daycare had an overall 6 to 1 ratio, but the Infant Room was a 4 to 1 ratio. If you place your child in a daycare, consider asking what room they will be in and what the child-to-staff ratio is in that particular room. I would also ask what the different rooms are and what the age-ranges are of the children in each room.

Some daycares provide curriculum for the kids, whereas in others, the kids just play all day. You will need to decide if you want your child to have work to do or if playing should be the only thing on the schedule. Once you know what you want for your child, then ask the staff about it. What does a typical day in the Infant Room look like? Do the kids do activities? Do they put the kids down for naps? What time is nap time? Where do they nap? Do they have snack time? Who provides the snacks? If your child is older and should be starting preschool, what does the educational curriculum look like? Do they get homework? What happens if your child is behind in math or reading? Does the curriculum adjust to his or her educational needs? What if your child is gifted and advanced? Will the daycare provide your child with material that will stimulate his or her mind? It might seem crazy to start thinking about this kind of thing now, but childhood goes by quickly and the schooling years are just around the corner.

There is another topic to consider when thinking about putting your child in a daycare, and that is discipline. How does this facility plan to enforce the rules with your child? Do they spank? Do they give time-outs, and if they do, how are the time-outs given? Are privileges taken away? Are they lectured? Is discipline conducted in front of the other children or is it conducted in private? Who is the disciplinarian? How are you, the parent, notified that your child misbehaved?

You may not know what is "ok" in terms of discipline for a daycare. Every state has different laws. I would encourage you to look into what the "norm" is in your area, what the state laws are around disciplining children, and then decide if you are ok with this procedure for discipline. Then, ask your proposed daycare what they do and how they go about doing it. If it fits your ideas, great! If not, see if they would be willing to modify their procedures for you and your child. If the answer is "No," time to look elsewhere.

Finally, if you are going to put your child in a daycare, please make sure they are certified and licensed. Double and triple check, please! Look to see if there have been any formal complaints brought against the facility, and if there has, then look into it. Also, do not feel afraid to ask how the daycare's hiring process works. Does the staff have a formal background check performed? Are their fingerprints taken and checked to make sure there are no felonies or serious crimes committed by the potential staff member on their record? This is your child and you have a right to know this type of information. So ask!

My final tip about daycares is to start looking early. Something I quickly learned when I was shopping around for Rachel is that the really good ones fill up fast! I remember that one of the daycares by my home had a 1 year waiting list. One full year! If you wait until the last minute to look for a daycare, you might find yourself stuck with one that you don't like or are uncomfortable with. I started shopping for daycares in November of 2013, expecting to start Rachel in August of 2014. When I found the place I wanted, I placed a deposit down to reserve her spot for the following year. Really good preschools and daycares will have a waiting list, no doubt about it. So shop early!

Shopping for a daycare can be overwhelming. In order to help you, I created a Daycare Interview Guide that you can print out and use as often as you need. As a bonus, when your child is ready to start elementary school, you'll be able to use this same guide to find the best school for you. You can check it out at:

www.kcdreisbach.com/daycare-school-interview-guide

Babysitters & Nannies

Babysitters and nannies are an odd category because it varies so much in what you should expect and look for. For example, if the babysitter came from an agency, then you can ask many of the same questions that I listed above for daycares, including what the hiring process looks like. You can also hire a babysitter on a day you are already home. Then, you can see how the babysitter interacts with your child, and how she or he handles different problems that might come up, including issues revolving around discipline. You can check for licenses and certifications too, and see if there have been any formal complaints.

If you are hiring a babysitter from an advertisement or looking for local college or high school students, then things become a little trickier because you have less to look at to reassure yourself that you made a good choice. Furthermore, high school and college students have to go to school during the week too, so they may not be a very viable option unless you are considering them for the summer. If you do decide to try a high school or college student as a babysitter, check for the basics like, do they know how to change a diaper? Do they know how to prepare breastmilk or formula? Do they have previous experience and what was it? Ask for references and call them. Some cities offer babysitting classes where they teach kids how to babysit younger children. You may consider asking your potential babysitter if they've taken such a class and how long ago they completed it. You can also hire the student for the day and see how he/she interacts with your child while you are home to observe them.

Regardless of the type of babysitter, there is a nice advantage that you may or may not get at a daycare: You get to implement your own schedule! Since you are paying someone to watch your baby, you can request, as a condition of their employment, that they follow your child's schedule. So, if your child is on a special diet, such as all organic and non-processed foods, or if your child naps exactly at ten o'clock in the morning and only for one hour, or goes on a walk every day at one o'clock, etc., you can request this and expect it to happen. If it does not happen, then you have a right to find someone else who will follow through with your requests. Please be patient with the babysitter, however, especially if you have a stubborn or spirited child. If you have a hard time getting your kid to follow your schedule or rules, then your babysitter will too!

Knowing that your baby is following the routine you put together for her will often ease a parent's mind when they go back to work. I remember frequently finding out that Rachel was just starting to go down for a nap at two o'clock in the evening when she should have been waking up at that hour. It would frustrate me so much because I already knew that I was going to have a hard time getting her to go to bed that night due to a late nap. But the days that went according to Rachel's schedule were days that I felt more relaxed about being away from her. So I can honestly say that knowing your child is following the schedule you have mapped out for him or her will certainly help in easing the guilt and frustration of being at work. This is a great advantage to this option!

Caregivers

Caregivers are an awesome thing to have, and you should feel truly blessed and lucky if you have this as a childcare option when you go back to work. The nice thing about caregivers is that you already know their background, you know their disciplining styles, and you know you can trust them. Overall, there is less investigation needed, less research required, and less worry on your part. If you're like me, you will also feel less guilty because you know that your child is safe and spending time with someone he or she already knows (like grandma or grandpa). But caregivers come with their own set of frustrations and anxieties that you will experience if this is your chosen path.

As a therapist, one of the big things I had to learn about was child development and parenting techniques. The professor of my child development class stated one day a very important fact that most caregivers do not know:

If you care for a child for 40% of the week or more, then you are a PRIMARY caregiver. This means that you are also responsible for PARENTING that child.

This means that as a primary caregiver, they need to discipline the same way and maintain the same routine that you (as the parent) have already established. If your child is being cared for by a caregiver that has him or her 40% of the time or more, please feel free to hand this book over to them so that they can read the bolded statement for themselves.

The above statement is a very important fact, and unfortunately, is one of the trickiest parts of using caregivers as your primary childcare. Most of the time, caregivers tend to be grandparents, and grandparents are a wonderful aspect of your child's life. Most grandparents, however, are done with parenting. In fact, many grandparents believe their job is to give your kid brownies, cookies, and candies for breakfast and lunch, and then send them back to you on a huge sugar-rush. They want to spoil them, not discipline them. After all, they had to discipline you for 18 years. Why would they want to do that again? If the grandparent/caregiver has the child only a couple of times a week, then brownies for breakfast isn't a big deal. It *does* become a big deal when they are a primary caregiver, however, and this is when the frustration begins.

One of the saddest days I had at work was when I truly realized that my parents were raising Rachel, not me. The only lucky thing I had was that my parents seemed to respect my choices and tried their best to follow my rules. My dad was a good disciplinarian and very over-protective, which I would rather have than a laid-back caregiver who allowed my child to run amuck and get into all kinds of dangerous situations. My parents were also very good about asking permission from me for just about everything they did with Rachel, which I highly appreciated. Even though it might not have been a big deal that they took her to the park or took her to a museum, it made me feel like I still had a say in what my child did during the day, and this was important to me.

There were times when others would watch Rachel for me, and I remember feeling frustrated when I found out later that they had taken her out without telling me or asking my permission. Again, it may not have been that big of a deal that they took her to the aquarium, zoo, etc., but it meant that I didn't know where my baby was. What if there had been an emergency? What if I wanted to be the first person to see the expression on her face when she saw a giant elephant for the first time? For a while, I thought I was being overly sensitive, so I asked other women and men about their opinions on this topic, and what I found was that most have a huge problem with this and their caregivers.

Because caregivers tend to be someone you know personally, they automatically tend to think they have certain unspoken permissions or allowances with your child. They tend to think things like, *"She'll be fine with it."* My one girlfriend told me that her mother-in-law took her son to Disneyland without asking her, and my girlfriend thought he was home all day long. When she came home early from work to find the house empty, she called and found out they were just getting off of a ride. Even though she had taken her son to Disneyland several times before, she found herself extremely annoyed that no one asked her about it or even thought to mention it! Because it was her mother-in-law that did it, you bet her and her husband had one of the biggest fights in their marriage that night when he got home from work.

Apart from taking your baby out on a well-meaning trip to the zoo without asking you, the other big complaint I got from parents was that caregivers would not follow their schedule or parenting style. Whether it is because they did not believe in schedules or because they were too busy, they just didn't. When I told my mother-in-law I was going to write this book, she said to me, "You should talk about how everyone parents differently because the way I parent and you parent are different." And she was absolutely right! And this is the crux of the problem with caregivers, and this problem seems to be a widespread one too.

My one girlfriend said that her husband wanted their new baby to eat purely organic foods. Her caregiver was her mother, and she told her husband that they could not expect her mother to buy purely organic foods because it was too costly and hard to find. Next, he wanted the baby to follow an Eat-Play-Sleep routine, which my girlfriend also shut down, saying "Babe, my mom has her own chores to get done, errands, and crap she has to take care of. If we were paying her, ok, we can ask her to do this stuff, but she's doing this for free!" And that is exactly the issue with caregivers. You are not paying them… and because you are not paying them, which tends to be that the baby follows their schedule, not the other way around (i.e. the caregiver following your schedule/parenting style).

Given this information, I remind us that if your caregiver is a primary caregiver, then you need to establish some agreement with them on how your child should be parented, fed, and disciplined. If your caregiver does not agree with you, then you either need to find another option or you will have to make do with what you have available.

With all of this said, please remember that, despite the frustrations of these problems with caregivers, caregivers really are a blessing. They raised you, grew up with you, or have supported you in some way, and you turned out just fine. Your baby will be fine in their hands and you need to trust that everything is going to be ok. Remember, too, that you have every right to be upset and frustrated about the kind of stuff listed here. You are a parent, and you are a good parent, and that is why you care so much. If you didn't love and care for your baby, then you wouldn't be freaking out, and you wouldn't want to be so involved in your child's every day activities. As the parent of that child, you have a right to be asked permission and to know where your child is when he or she is not with you. Do not ever stop requesting these things from your caregiver, because in the end, all you are asking for is a little respect… respect for being that baby's mama or daddy.

4. THE TRIALS OF SEPARATION ANXIETY

Once you have figured out your childcare, there's a great possibility you will encounter separation anxiety. It doesn't matter if you work fulltime, part-time, or if you get to stay home with your child, separation anxiety is something most kids face. (And, if by some miracle you have no idea what I'm talking about, then start kissing the ground because you are LUCKY!) So, let's jump into this and figure out what, exactly, is "separation anxiety"?

Between the ages of approximately 18 months and 3 years of age, children may develop clinging behaviors toward a parent or caregiver. You may notice your little one crying when you leave the room or drop them off at Grandma's. When they realize you've gone, they become fearful that you may not be coming back, and so, crying ensues. Rest assured, friend, that your child is fine and completely normal. Typically, the crying will end once they become engaged in another activity. This type of anxiety is completely normal.

There is a point when separation anxiety, however, can become a diagnosable, mental health condition. In the past, I have had many parents come to me, curious to know if their child was suffering from Separation Anxiety Disorder (SAD). This is a mental health condition recognized by the American Psychiatric Association (APA) and is classified in the fifth edition of the Diagnostic Statistical Manual of Mental Health Disorders (DSM-5). The answer was almost always, *No*. When a mental health professional diagnoses a child with SAD, the child is usually between the ages of 7 and 9, and frequently struggles to calm down when the parent leaves them[1]. The child's grief is so intense that daycares or babysitters will frequently call the parent to come back and pick up the child. Eventually, the situation can deteriorate to the point where the parent may even lose their job! So, unless you find yourself living in the presence of your child at all times in order to avoid a catastrophic melt down, chances are that your child doesn't suffer from SAD.

Normal separation anxiety, however, can be very difficult to deal with. And I'm not just talking about your child's separation anxiety… but yours as well! Parents can suffer from this too, and it's just as heart-wrenching!

---

[1] "Childhood Anxiety Disorders." *Anxiety and Depression Association of America*, Sept. 2015, https://www.adaa.org/ livingwithanxiety/ children/childhood-anxiety-disorders. Accessed 19 April 2017.

I'll never forget the first day that I dropped Rachel off at daycare. I had pumped myself up and given myself one heck of a pep talk before taking her to the car and strapping her into her car-seat. I had taken the entire day off of work, wanting to be available to the daycare in case something went wrong. She and I strode in, signed the log book, and I watched as she tentatively moved into the room. As she became engaged in playing, I remember thinking, *Wow... this isn't so bad.* I gave her a kiss and a good, mamma-bear hug, and told her I would be back in two hours to pick her up. She just smiled and nodded. So I stood up and walked out. That's when the crying started.

Oh my goodness did she cry! She sobbed! She wailed! And then I heard those words that just stabbed my heart every time she gasped them, *"Mommy! Come back!"* What did I do? I came back, of course! The sounds of her blood curdling cries sent me racing back to the door to save her. I hugged her, kissed her, and reassured her that I was here and would be back shortly. She stopped crying and went back to playing. Once I started for the door, there went the crying again, *"Mommy!"*

This whole routine went on for a good five minutes before one of the daycare staff, ever-so-kindly, gestured me to the door. I got the hint... I wasn't helping. So I left, listening to Rachel's wails kicking up once again. That's when my own separation anxiety kicked in. Would she be ok? Will they take good care of her? Is she going to sob in a cold and lonely corner of the room for the whole two hours that I'm gone?

Every possible fear I had played out in my mind's eye like a terrible black-and-white film. I witnessed every single atrocity I had ever heard about played out towards my child in my mind. I was overwhelmed! So I did what every sensible parent in my situation would do… I hid in the bushes. Yes, you read that right. I hid in the bushes on the outside of the school fence. I shimmied my way into a bush, and camped out to watch how the daycare staff took care of my little Rachel.

I watched as they picked her up and comforted her, as they distracted her with toys and games, and as they sang her songs. I sat in that bush, which I came to know very well, for about an hour. And I would have stayed there longer too, but as it turns out, I'm not very stealthy. My cell phone rang, causing me to jump, smacking the fence. That fence clanged and rang out, gloriously announcing my presence as the creepiest and craziest mother in town!

I was not caught, thank goodness! Or else I would probably have enrolled her in a different daycare out of sheer embarrassment! I left and I called my sister, who consoled me as I cried and shared my frustrations with her. In the end, everything was fine. I picked Rachel up and she started again the following day. I battled that separation anxiety for quite some time, but eventually conquered it.

So, I hope you enjoyed my embarrassing tale, and that you won't feel quite as stupid as I did if you find yourself in a similar situation (like hiding in a bush). I certainly wouldn't judge you. My experience highlights how both, ourselves as parents and our children, will suffer from separation anxiety at some point. The question now becomes, how do we manage separation anxiety? Following below are some tips on how to manage this tough milestone. These tips will also help you adjust to leaving your child in the arms of a new childcare situation too!

Tip #1: Prepare for the Big Day

Preparation is key for young children. Letting them know what the plan is and what time to expect different transitions helps to ease a child's anxiety levels. This is also true for you. Take the time to visit the childcare facility (or the home of the caregiver) at least once before the first day. Bring your child along with you and highlight the things your Little One can look forward to. For example, if there is a playground, take them to see it and say things like, *"Doesn't that playhouse look like fun? Wouldn't it be nice to go and play in there?"* Or, *"Look at these cool blocks! Wouldn't it be nice to build a tower with them?"* Doing this helps to create a visual memory for your child of something that they like or are interested in within this new environment. While you visit, keep reminding your child that this is where they will be coming to play while you go to work (or class, run errands, etc.).

When you are checking out the place with your child, introduce them to their new caregiver too. Give them time to meet the primary person (or people) who will be responsible for them in your absence. Get the individual's name and try to build a working relationship with them. Children, especially young children, will often look to their parents to learn how to react to a new person or situation. If they see you smiling and laughing with this new caregiver, that gives your child the signal that this person is "ok" in your book.

If your child is already potty trained, take your child to the bathroom at the childcare facility. Show them where it is located and let them use the bathroom if they have to go. If there is a spot where the children nap, take your child there too. Show them where he or she will be sleeping and what they will be sleeping on. Finally, if there is a cubby or special place where your child's belongings will go (like their jacket, bed sheets, etc.), show them that as well, letting them know that the cubby will be their little space for keeping their items safe. All of this helps to make the new environment more familiar and less scary for your kids. I also believe it makes it less scary for us as parents too.

Tip #2: No Sneaking Out!

Just about every parent I know is guilty of sneaking out on their baby or child at some point or another. Usually we sneak out because we believe that if they don't see us leave they won't experience grief. Unfortunately, this is faulty logic. Our children will always notice our absence, and when they realize we have left, will most likely become disheartened and experience their separation anxiety. What's more, sneaking out usually produces more fear in the child. Children start to lose their trust in a parent who is always sneaking out on them. As a result, when you start to say things like, *"I'll pick you up later,"* they won't believe you.

It is important that we always tell our children the truth. If we are dropping them off with Grandma and we won't be coming back for an hour, then we need to say exactly that to them. Be honest. Let them know that you are leaving and when you will be back. Don't sneak out! Even if your child is happily engaged in another activity, still catch his attention and tell him that you are leaving. Trust me with this one…. Everyone thinks sneaking out is the more "humane" way of handling it. The reality is, however, that sneaking out is easier for *you* because you don't have to experience your child's tears. Although it is easier for you, it is just as hard on your child (if not worse!) as you kissing them and saying goodbye.

Tip #3: Call for Reinforcements

Remember in Tip #1 how I told you to introduce your child to the primary person responsible for him? This is when you call that person in. Sometimes, you might find that your Little One just can't let go of you. And you might discover that your own separation anxiety and feelings of guilt keep you from just walking away. Now is the time to call for help. Walk your child over to that person and hand them off. Let's explore this a bit further….

There were some days that Rachel went to daycare just fine. Sometimes, however, she struggled. I noticed these incidents occurred when there were big changes that happened in our own lives, like moving to our new house. On days like this, where she struggled to transition to daycare, I would enlist help. There was a teacher who was always there in the morning. When Rachel would begin crying, I would walk us over to this teacher and let the teacher know that Rachel was having a hard time saying goodbye. This teacher was always so kind and would always take Rachel's hand from me saying, *"Do you want to go walk Mommy to the car and say goodbye?"* Rachel would, of course, say *yes.* So she would hold Rachel and walk with us to the gate at the edge of the property. Then she would prompt Rachel to say goodbye to me. That was my cue to give one final kiss and hug, and walk away. As I walked away, I would hear her engage Rachel in a conversation about something, and Rachel would happily chat away.

Handing Rachel over to someone she knew always helped on those more anxious days. As such, I really recommend giving this tactic a try. You can even speak to the staff member ahead of time, asking if they would be willing to be the person you hand your child off to on those difficult days.

Tip #4: Just Walk Away... No Lingering!

When our children cry, we have a natural instinct to want to fix things. We are drawn to their tears and wailings, even as our hair stands-on-end and our minds scream to run away! Our hearts pull us to the sound of their suffering, and we are instantly overwhelmed with the desire to protect them from everything. This parental instinct is a powerful and wonderful thing, but in the case of separation anxiety... not so much.

Remember my story towards the beginning of this chapter? Remember how every time Rachel cried out for me, I kept coming back? Eventually, the daycare staff very nicely hinted to me that it was time to leave. They explained that lingering at "goodbye time" only makes it worse. Although our parental instinct tells us to remain with our child, in this situation, we are doing more harm than good. As a therapist, I knew that this was true, but as a Mom, I was struggling with accepting this reality. That's why I hid in the bushes.

Although hiding in the foliage of the playground turned me into a semi-crazed Helicopter Parent, I also got to witness how my daughter was able to calm down shortly after I left. Lingering around after you say goodbye actually prolongs your child's cries. If you give your hugs and kisses quickly, say your goodbyes, and then leave, your child will spend less time crying and more time enjoying his or her environment. This doesn't mean that you ignore his concerns. Rather, you address them and then confidently move along with the plan you have created. I'll give you an example:

> Tim is going to daycare for the first time today. His dad, Paul, made sure to take a tour of the daycare with Tim, noted some fun toys Tim might like to play with, and introduced Tim to Ms. Kathy, one of the daycare staff. When Dad goes to say goodbye, Tim begins to cry, clinging to his father's leg and begging him not to go. Paul gently gives Tim a hug and says, *"I know you don't want me to leave, but I have to go to work right now. You're going to stay here and play while I go to work. Remember those blocks we saw yesterday? You get to play with those while I am gone, ok?"* Tim nods, acknowledging that this idea of playing with the blocks is an intriguing one, as he wipes the tears from his face, his bottom lip puckered out.

> Although Tim seems a little more at ease, Paul can tell that his son is not convinced. So he tries another tactic, *"I'll tell you what. Let's find Ms. Kathy. There she is. Ms. Kathy, I need to leave for*

work now, but Tim is having a hard time. I know he was interested in playing with those blocks. Would you be willing to play blocks with him while I leave for work?" Ms. Kathy smiles and nods, taking Tim's hand and prompting him to wave goodbye to Paul. She then leads Tim away. Tim begins crying again, shouting for his Dad. Paul replies, *"I love you! I will pick you back up after you have had Nap Time,"* and then turns and walks away.

In this example, Paul is not fooled... he knows that Tim is upset about him leaving and none of our Tips have worked. Instead of lingering on, however, he quickly makes his exit. Paul doesn't ignore Tim's sadness or feelings, and he tries to pass Tim on to someone he knows, helping to reduce Tim's anxiety. This is how all of these tips work together to ease the transition into a new caregiver situation. They may not always prevent your child's tears, but I promise that they *are* working to <u>reduce</u> the fear and anxiety.

Tip #5: Have a Drop-Off Routine & Be Consistent

Much of the reason why a new caregiver situation produces so much anxiety for children is because it is a break from the normal routine. Children thrive on a routine, and while some bounce back from a change in plan rather easily, others really struggle whenever there is an adjustment made. Although being consistent won't help in the immediate moment that you separate from your child, consistency helps in the long run. By being consistent when and how you say your goodbyes, you start creating a new routine that your child can look forward to for comfort. If Paul, in the previous example, always says goodbye and then hands Tim off to Ms. Kathy, then Tim will begin to understand that the moment Ms. Kathy comes into the picture, it means it is time to transition into the daycare routine. This, in turn, will reduce the anxiety Tim feels. The more a child knows the game plan, the better they will be able to transition from one activity to another with little or no anxiety. So, develop a little ritual or routine that your child can follow when it's time to be dropped off at daycare. It can be simple, just be consistent about applying it at drop-off. The consistency will truly be an asset in soothing your child's anxiety.

I remember that there was this young boy at Rachel's school who started a few months after she did. He would sob whenever his father dropped him off, and it wasn't getting any better, even after a few weeks of being at the school. One day, I came to drop Rachel off and saw the Dad putting a puzzle together with his son on the floor of the daycare. When the puzzle was done, he gave his son a kiss, said goodbye, and left. This time, his son didn't cry when Dad left. The following day, the same thing happened. They did a puzzle together, the father then left for work, and his son didn't cry.

This Dad had created a ritual for his son. He brought him to the school a little earlier so that they could complete this puzzle together and would consistently leave afterwards. This new little routine of putting the puzzle together served as a *transition* for this child. It helped this boy mentally prepare himself for Dad leaving. And since Dad was consistent about it, it was very effective in eliminating the child's anxiety about being dropped off. No more crying or clinging behaviors! Eventually, the Dad slowly stopped doing this routine, transitioning out of completing the puzzle until he no longer had to do this part of the routine. And the child was fine; he had finally adjusted to his new childcare environment. This Dad did a great job and he illustrates a perfect example of what a little drop-off routine can look like.

Tip #6: Use a Transitional Object...
if You Have Too

Some kids just need a little extra something to help them switch over into a new environment. Do you remember when your Tot was a baby? Maybe he had a special blanket that he would cling to at night when you turned off the light? Or perhaps he had a stuffed animal that he loved dearly and would drag all around the house? Most people call these items a "lovey." A lovey can be very useful when transitioning your child into a new environment. This is why, in the field of psychology, we call a "lovey" a "transitional object," because the object helps the individual transition into a new environment or stage of life.

Offering your child a toy or a blanket that he loves to take to daycare as a *transitional object* may help your Little One transition from one environment to the other. It gives them a sense of comfort and helps the child feel a little less alone. Remember, even though they may be surrounded by children, they don't know anyone, making them feel lonely. This feeling of loneliness contributes to their fear and anxiety. Having a lovey that they can cling to will help them feel a little less lonely and a little less scared.

Leaving your baby or tot in a new environment is a scary and heart-wrenching experience. It can leave both you and your child feeling overwhelmed, emotionally exhausted, and physically drained. Hang in there… it does get better! As you and your child get accustomed to the new routine, you will both feel more confident in your abilities to manage the situation. The increase in confidence will help you feel better as a parent and will help your child feel better in managing new situations too.

Conquering this scary transition will truly help your Little One in discovering their own abilities to self-sooth, seek help if needed, and simply, begin the process of discovering who he or she is as an individual, separate from you! They know who they are as your child (i.e. "I'm Tim, the son of Paul"), but who are they apart from that? (i.e. "I'm Tim. But Paul's not here. So who am I now?") It is my belief that this is part of the "scariness" of separating from a parent. As a child, much of their identity comes from you and who *you* say they are. When you are removed from the equation, there is a hole… an empty space left to fill. That's scary. What will fill that hole?

Over time, your child will experiment with filling this hole with other things, such as friends, other adults, hobbies/interests, clubs, sports, and other external activities outside of the home. All of this begins to help shape the identity your child will carry (i.e. I'm Tim, son of Paul. But I'm also Tanya's friend, and Ms. Kathy's helper, and a really good paper-cutter"). This identity will continue to morph and shape itself as they get older, but it all starts here. So hang in there. It'll all be ok.

5. BREASTFEEDING & THE WORKPLACE

When Rachel was born, I hemorrhaged two hours after her delivery and lost about two liters of blood, according to my doctors. This was not including what I had already lost during labor and delivery. I was anemic, but I really wanted to breastfeed. My in-laws were champion breastfeeders, and I am pretty sure that they could have kept an army fed through any food shortage if the need arose. My husband's grandmother was also a nurse and a lactation consultant, and so she was also very pro-breastfeeding. Naturally, I felt a lot of pressure to breastfeed and to get it right. I also really wanted too, so their successes were great motivations for me to keep going.

Due to the anemia from the blood loss, breastfeeding was really hard for me to get started; my body was way too focused on making blood instead of milk. As such, Rachel was supplemented in the beginning with formula while I pumped and tried to convince my body to make baby food. [**Side Note:** If anyone tells you that breastfeeding does not hurt if you are doing it right, don't listen. They are lying! I had three lactation consultants and Champion Milk-Makers (aka my in-laws) tell me that I was "doing it right" and that Rachel's latch was "perfect," and I still bled from my nipples and was in pain for two weeks! But, if you can make it past those first two weeks, it is instantly better. I promise!] Rachel breastfed for about four months before she transitioned completely to a bottle (long story here), but before she did, I went back to work and pumped milk.

Now, because this book is about working and parenting, I thought breastfeeding should be covered, at least a little bit. Many women choose not to breastfeed, and there is nothing wrong with this choice. There are many, very good reasons to choose bottle-feeding or formula over nursing. Those moms that choose to breastfeed, however, find that they have a hard time managing breastfeeding and going back to work. Most breastfeeding books cover this topic very well, though, so I highly recommend that you pick up a book on breastfeeding in order to gain more information and ideas on how to manage breastfeeding and the workplace. But I did want to run through a few things quickly before we moved on to other topics.

Expressing Milk in the Workplace

I mentioned that I went back to school two weeks after Rachel was born. My university provided me with a professor's office for me to use for expressing milk. I would request the key from the secretary, put a sign on the door saying "Privacy Please," and then locked the door. When I was done, I would take the sign down and give the key back to the secretary. When I went to work, I had my own office. So I would lock the door and put a sign out saying "Do Not Disturb," and then would unlock it when I was done. I had a lunchbox with ice packs that I would use to store the milk until I got home. If I could, I would put the lunchbox in the fridge at work or at school to ensure the milk was staying cold enough.

Now, I am not well versed on the laws of other states or countries, but my recommendation is to look them up and become familiar with them if you plan to pump milk at work. Your next step should be to inform your boss that you need a private space, assuming you don't already have access to one, like a private office. Make sure you have a good pump, a lunchbox with ice packs to store the milk in case you do not have a refrigerator at work, and supplies to clean the pump accessories if you do not have access to a kitchen where you can clean things off with soap and water. Medela makes some great products for breastfeeding, including special wipes that sanitize the accessories if you do not have access to a sink (i.e. Medela Quick Clean Wipes). Go to your local baby store and check out the breastfeeding section to see what is out there today to make your life easier at work.

Breastfeeding can also be awkward at work because you are not home, your breasts are exposed to the air, and, psychologically, you know your boobs should not be hanging out in the workplace. Nonetheless, this is the reality of breastfeeding and working. I never had this particular problem, but many of my girlfriends said they had a hard time letting down milk at work. Some suggestions they gave if you are having this problem is to bring a picture of your baby to work, have something that smells like your baby with you, or have a video on your phone of your baby doing something adorable. They also highly recommended the use of breast pads in case you can't pump as soon as you were hoping to and begin leaking milk. With that said, I would also keep an extra shirt at work in case you have a milk-related accident. There is nothing worse than having to walk around with two giant milk stains where your nipples are in the employee lunch room!

A final recommendation is something that I figured out the hard way. You will find one day that you are running late and you are trying desperately to remember everything: what the baby needs for her day at daycare, your lunch, the milk lunchbox, the ice packs, your purse, your sweater, etc. You get to work, your breasts are horribly engorged because you couldn't pump sooner, and you finally have the chance. You close the door, sit down, go to pull out your pump and then realize you forgot it at home. What do you do now?

If you are lucky, you live close enough to home to swing by and use it. If you are unlucky, as I was, you live 45 minutes away and there is no way you will make it there and back before your break is over. My recommendation and the solution to this problem? You buy two pumps. I know, pumps are expensive, but so is the cost of formula! I was lucky enough that there was a Target in the shopping center where my office was. So I went and bought a single-electric pump. It did not cost me too much (about $40), and although it was not nearly as good as my double-electric pump at home, it did the job and got me through the day. After that, I always kept that little pump in my car and I am grateful I did because not too long after that, I forgot my big pump at home again and I had to rely on the little one to get me through once more. At the very least, consider registering for it… you never know, someone just might get it for you!

A final option is to learn how to manually express breastmilk. This is not the best solution in any way because it is actually really difficult to express milk from your breast using only your hands. Nevertheless, it is certainly an option that can work in a pinch. You can find several diagrams online that will teach the proper technique for expressing milk this way. Be sure to learn these techniques well to avoid damaging breast tissue, or speak to a lactation consultant to learn from them directly on how to use these techniques correctly.

A Special Note for Moms who Can't or Choose Not to Breastfeed

When my older sister had her first son, she worked very hard to breastfeed. He was a month early, had a poor latch, and a weak suck. After months of diligent efforts to breastfeed her baby began to lose weight and he was not meeting his expected weight gains or growth. This was a very scary time for her, and after a long battle, she gave up. I remember sitting with her one day as she cried. She felt like a failure.

It is an awful experience, to wait so long for your baby to arrive, to be told over and over again about how wonderful breastfeeding is, to feel the pressure of needing to provide your Little One with the best nutrients you can possibly provide, and then to find out that you just can't…. What if you *can* breastfeed but work, lack of time, or simply a baby who becomes spoiled off the bottle, causes you to throw out your breastfeeding dreams? What a terrible guilty feeling overcomes you! I remember, I went through that too.

Rachel became spoiled off the bottle (a very long story here), and eventually refused to latch on completely. I remember feeling so frustrated, annoyed, and depressed that I gave it up all together! I stopped breastfeeding cold turkey and Rachel began to drink formula. But I was so sad that I had to quit early. Even *looking* at the breast pump would make me cry! So I bagged it up and insisted my sister take it from me, even though she was not pregnant yet. I felt like a failure too….

How many women go through this? Feeling guilty, ashamed, or feeling like terrible mothers simply because they can't or choose not to breastfeed. I am here to tell you that it is ok. Being unable to or choosing not to breastfeed does NOT make you a bad mother. (And to the husbands who just might be reading this book, it does not make your partner a bad mom!) Breastfeeding, though great for your baby, is only good when both mother *and* baby want to do it!

If you are stressing out every time the baby cries for milk, or your Little One sobs because he can't latch properly or, for some reason, he is not getting enough milk at your breast, is it really worth it? Is it worth resenting your baby or your baby going hungry because he refuses to breastfeed? No, no it's not. Although breastmilk is amazing for your baby, and there is no true substitute for it, it is in no way worth you or your baby suffering! Psychologically speaking, it is more important that you and your baby enjoy mealtime together in a stress-free setting rather than you gritting your teeth, crying, or feeling anger during these precious moments. Cut yourself some slack and tune out anyone who might be pressuring you to breastfeed. Your baby will be just fine, and so will you.

A Special Note & Tips for "Exclusively Pumping" Moms

I mentioned my sister who had to stop breastfeeding because her little boy was struggling too much. Although she could not breastfeed my nephew, she decided to do the next best thing: exclusively pump. To "exclusively pump" means that you do not breastfeed and you do not formula feed. You bottle feed your baby your expressed breast milk. It is very similar to the Working Breastfeeding Mom because you have to pump and store milk (unlike a Stay-at-Home-Mom who usually does not pump because she can simply put the baby to the breast at any given time), but you also go through all the bottle-feeding stuff a Formula Mom does. It is kind of a hybrid of these two lifestyles, I suppose, but also is its very own crazy beast. Here is why:

An Exclusively Pumping Mom may not be able to put the baby to the breast when it is time to eat (usually because breastfeeding was not successful). So, she needs to feed the baby, which means thawing or warming up breast milk, preparing a bottle, and burping the baby during and after the feeding. After the baby is fed, she then needs to pump to make sure she maintains her milk supply, which entails preparing the breast pump, pumping, storing milk in the fridge/freezer, and cleaning the pump and associated materials afterwards. Although Working Breastfeeding Moms have to do all the pumping stuff, they generally do not have to feed the baby too at the same time. They are at work! And when they are home, they just put the baby to the breast like the Stay-At-Home Breastfeeding Mom does.

Furthermore, when the Exclusively Pumping Mom goes out on an errand with the baby, she has the added ordeal of not only feeding the baby, but having to pump while out and about as well because she can't simply "put the baby to the breast." As such, Exclusively Pumping Moms might feel a little more home-bound or feel much more governed by the clock because they need to be able to find a place to pump every couple of hours. The Formula Mom just whips out the bottle and the Breastfeeding Mom (regardless of working or not) just whips out the breast when lunch time comes around for their babies.

I have a lot of respect for the Exclusively Pumping Mom because her actions display a lot of diligence and commitment to her baby. It was not until my sister decided to exclusively pump that I even realized this category of "mom" even existed! I remember talking to her one day about my plans to write this book, and one of her recommendations (or maybe it was more of a request) was to make sure that in the chapter on breastfeeding, I include the Exclusively Pumping Mom. At the time, she was part of a Mom's Support group, and she shared that Exclusively Pumping Moms feel excluded from breastfeeding books, blogs, and support groups. At first, I thought, *"Well, it is just like a Working Breastfeeding Mom, isn't it?"* But later, after watching her and seeing the hoops she had to jump through, I realized that the Exclusively Pumping Mom is in a category all on her own, and she deserves to be included too!

If you are a mom who exclusively pumps, many of the tips I listed earlier in this chapter will work for you. There are, however, some additional ones that other Exclusively Pumping Moms wanted me to share with you too:

Tip #1: Consider Taking Supplements

One of the biggest struggles Exclusively Pumping Moms will face is maintaining their milk supply. Breast Pumps are not perfect and can never perfectly replicate a baby's suck. As such, many women, over time, find that their milk supply begins to diminish because the pump is not completely emptying their breasts (thus signaling to the body to produce a little less milk each time). As such, aside from making sure you are drinking plenty of fluids, you should also consider taking herbal supplements that will help maintain, and potentially increase, your milk supply. There are many out on the market today, but my lactation consultant had recommended Blessed Thistle and Fenugreek. These are the supplements my sister took as well, and they were wonderfully effective for her. You may follow the directions on the bottle, but most breast-milk producing women find they need more than directed on the bottle. As such, please consult with your local lactation consultant, or potentially your OB-GYN, on dosages.

Tip #2: Get a GOOD Pump

Pivotal to your success as an Exclusively Pumping

Mom is a REALLY GOOD PUMP! Unfortunately, you just can't afford to go cheap. The better the pump, the more likely you will be successful in completely emptying out your breasts. At the time when I had Rachel, Medela was highly known for great quality breast pumps. My sister used mine, which was a Medela, 2006 Pump In Style Advanced. It worked wonderfully for her. You might also check with your health insurance to see if you qualify for renting (potentially for free) a hospital-grade breast pump. It does not get any better than a hospital-grade pump, so check into it.

Tip #3: Go with a Double Electric

There are a couple of different options when it comes to breast pumps. There are manual pumps, which you pump (You guessed it!) manually, and then there are electric pumps, which you simply plug in and turn on. Once you have figured out manual versus electric, you have more options to choose from: you can go with a "single" pump or a "double." A "single" pump allows you to pump only one breast at a time, whereas a "double" allows you to pump both breasts at the same time. Usually, manual pumps are single pumps and double pumps are electric pumps, but I have seen a few the other way around. The big recommendation here is to buy a double electric pump, and here is why: TIME! As a new parent, and one with a career no doubt, time is always of the essence! Electric pumps are not only more efficient at emptying your breasts completely, but they are also faster in general. And of course, if you are pumping both breasts at once, then you are really speeding through it… sort of (it still takes 20-30 minutes). So, if you can afford it, go with a double electric pump.

Tip #4: Get a Car Adapter & a Battery Pack

Remember how I said that an Exclusively Pumping Mom might feel a little more home-bound? Well a car adapter or a battery pack can really help with this problem if you have an electric pump. The car adapter allows the breast pump to be used in the car. So if you are at the park with your baby and the time comes to pump, you can climb into the security of your car, plug in your pump, and get to it! The battery pack is also convenient because it allows you to use your pump off of batteries. So, if your toddler refuses to get off the swings, but you need to pump, you can sit on the bench, cover yourself with a nursing blanket, and run the pump off of the battery pack. You pump and while avoiding the tantrum.

Tip #5: Get a Hands-Free Pumping Bra

I never had one of these, but my sister swore by it! This bra basically has flaps that you can insert the breast shields into (that is the part that goes around your nipple), and holds them in place while you pump. The effect is then that you have your hands available to do whatever it is you want. My sister was a teacher and a very busy woman, so she would grade papers, do dishes, read a book, cook, etc., while pumping! This little freedom can go a long way in helping you maintain your sanity and get things done on that tight and packed schedule of yours.

Tip #6: Have a Pumping Routine

A pumping routine is something any breastfeeding mom should consider. Whether you are pumping because you are at work, on vacation without the baby, or exclusively pumping, getting in all of those pumps can get tricky. If pumping isn't something you make time for in your day, you'll forget to do it and miss it completely.

The best suggestion for this is to simply add it into your daily routine. That doesn't mean that you have to have a specific pumping hour (i.e. at 9:00 a.m., I'm going to pump!). Rather, you should know what sequence the events of your day will follow, and where pumping will fall into that sequence.

You might be wondering why I am advising you to have a *routine* versus a *schedule* of events. With *scheduling*, you are essentially blocking out times for each item; so what's the harm in that? The truth is, there is no harm in it, but most people find that they don't schedule enough time for most things that need to get done. So, they become overwhelmed and frustrated with the fact that their day "didn't go as planned." Having a general sequence of events without set times makes your day feel a little more flexible. This is purely a psychological thing, however. So if you like having a set time for everything, then by all means, go for it! The important thing is just to make sure you develop a routine for pumping. However you want to do it is just fine.

6. YOUR SECOND JOB... HOME

To start this section, let us begin with a little story, a snippet into your potential life. See if you can identify yourself with one of these characters:

Lisa and Jim

Lisa found a solution to her childcare needs and has gone back to work. Today was particularly tough, dealing with the guilt and all, but she made it through and finally gets to go home and see her baby and toddler. She pulls into the driveway, gets into the house, looks at her watch and realizes it is five o' clock and her spouse, Jim, will be home any minute. Dinner needs to be made, baths need to be had, chores need to get done, some sort of quality time with the baby needs to get squeezed in, and the bedtime routine needs to all be completed by 8:00 p.m. That gives her three hours to manage it all. *No problem*, she thinks to herself, *I can do this!* She starts by getting the baby in the swing and the toddler watching a movie. She races to the kitchen and starts chopping up veggies, cooking rice, and getting meat sliced when the toddler shows up and wants her attention. "Not now Sweetie," she says, "Mommy needs to get dinner ready." He ignores her comment and continues pulling on her pant leg.

Now the baby starts crying. She is hungry and needs milk, but Lisa can't breastfeed because the food is cooking on the stove and it will burn if unattended for more than 5 minutes. But she can't let the baby go hungry either…. She decides to turn off the stove and feed the baby. The toddler follows her and starts trying to show Lisa his book, begging her to read to him. "Not now. Mommy will read to you after dinner."

He is jealous, of course, that she is giving the baby attention, so he persists, "No! Read now!" He begins having a meltdown as she denies him a third time.

At this point, Jim comes home to see the toddler screaming in a tantrum, and Lisa sitting, feeding the baby. Jim asks innocently, "Is dinner ready?"

Lisa begins to fume inside, completely frustrated and annoyed. "Does it look like it is ready?" she snaps.

"Calm down," he retorts back with a hint of annoyance, "I was just asking…. What is your problem?'" While Lisa continues to seethe inside, she realizes that it is 6:30 p.m. and dinner still isn't cooked. She yells at Jim to get the toddler to stop crying and watch the baby while she gets dinner going. He, begrudgingly, agrees. Lisa goes back to food preparations while he manages the kids.

Finally, dinner is done. Lisa gets plates on the table and Jim gets the baby in the high chair. It is 7:00 p.m. and the family is finally having dinner. Lisa starts to feed the baby again, when her toddler decides he wants to paint the table with his mashed potatoes. "Eat," Jim says firmly to his son.

The toddler replies, of course, "No!" Lisa tries to beg him to have at least one bite of food. "No! No like!" The toddler protests, and then he throws his food on the floor.

"Time-out," says Jim, who then chases the toddler around the house for a 2 minute time-out. Screaming and a tantrum start in the other room, scaring the baby, making her cry too. Lisa tries to soothe the baby. Eventually, everyone eats and calms down, but when Lisa looks at the clock, it is 7:45 p.m. *Yikes!* Baths should have been given over half an hour ago and the family is only, just now, finishing dinner! What happened to the time? So much for having it all done by 8:00 p.m.

Do you see how this story goes? I will not bother finishing it because I think you can manage to write the ending pretty well all on your own. Does it sound familiar at all? Maybe you only have one child, but you will be surprised to know that this story does not change much if you have one or three kids. The trials are the same, just a little trickier or a little longer. Essentially, you come home and there is A LOT to accomplish before your head hits a pillow at night, and most likely, you will not get all of those things done. So how do you manage it all? How do you go to work all day and still manage a household?

Dealing with Home-Life

Surprise, surprise, there are no easy answers on how to manage it all. I really wish I could give you a Super Maid to come to your house and take care of all the mundane stuff, but I can't. What I can do is give you a few ideas on how to make it a little easier on yourself. Many of my girlfriends had some great ideas I never thought of, and so I collected them and bring them to you here. Let us start with one of the most time consuming and very important tasks of home-life: cooking dinner!

Dinner, and family meals in general, are an important part of family time. There has been plenty of research over the past 15 years to show that family meals are important in childhood development. If you do not currently share meals at the table with your children, I highly encourage you to start doing so. I know it's hard… many times in my house we start off the week at the dinner table and slowly migrate to the sofa as the week moves on. But do try… even if for only one or two meals a week. If you want, think of it this way: sharing a meal together around a table is time you can count towards the "quality time" section of your night! Yay!

As mentioned, dinnertime is a central part of human

interaction, but how do we manage dinner when we only have a few hours to get everything in? The following tips have been gathered to help you do it all, including general household work, and be amazing at it!

Tip #1: Plan & Shop for Weekday Meals over the Weekend

One of the best suggestions given to me by working parents is to plan your meals out ahead of time. Every Sunday, one of my girlfriends lists out what dinner she will be making for each night of the week. She then forms a list of any groceries needed to make those meals happen and then she hits the grocery store with her kids in tow. Have you ever noticed how much time you spend trying to come up with something for dinner? And then when you finally figured out what you want (i.e. spaghetti and meatballs) you realize you do not have all the ingredients (i.e. meatballs!). Your option then is to hit the store after work or think of something else. The genius of planning meals for the week over the weekend is that you free up extra time during the week for family fun or chores.

Tip #2: Prepare Parts of the Meal over the Weekend

Another girlfriend of mine who plans meals over the weekend goes the extra step of prepping parts of each meal beforehand. This is another way to save tons of time during the work week, especially if you are busy with your kids in after school activities. For example, if my girlfriend is going to make spaghetti on Monday night, she preps the sauce over the weekend. Her kids are super picky eaters, and getting them to eat vegetables is a huge chore. So she tricks them into eating healthy! She heats up a jar of pasta sauce and then adds all kinds of pureed veggies (like squash, carrots, or spinach), cooks it all up and then stores it in the refrigerator for Monday (or the freezer for later on in the week). Not only do her kids lick their bowls clean because they enjoyed their dinner (yummy hidden veggies!), but she saves herself lots of time with mid-week cooking!

Another example of preparing meals over the weekend actually comes from my older sister, and it is truly a brilliant plan. Money can be tight when raising a family, so buying in bulk while stuff is on sale is very helpful. My sister buys meat/chicken in bulk when it goes on sale. She then prepares big batches of marinades on Sunday and will count out enough portions of chicken for everyone (i.e. 3 breasts for 3 people) and bag them in freezer zip-lock bags. (So, essentially, there would be three pieces of chicken in one zip-lock bag, and another three pieces of chicken in second zip-lock, etc.) She then divides out the marinade into the different bags, mixes it all up, and then freezes the chicken. The result is a juicy and tender chicken dish for quick weekday meals. Pull the meat out in the morning to thaw and then quickly pan fry it or cook it in the oven. Combine that with some frozen veggies cooked in the microwave and you have a quick, easy, and healthy dinner! Want to vary it up? Try this same idea with other meats, fish, and veggies too!

Tip #3: Batch Cooking

Batch cooking is a pretty simple idea and can be done at any time that you are preparing a meal (i.e. weekend or mid-week). When you have chosen to make a particular meal that is freezer friendly, such as a beef and barley stew, buy enough ingredients to double or triple your recipe. Cook the meal as you normally would, just in much larger quantities. Portion out the leftovers in zip-lock bags or freezer-safe containers and freeze for quick meals on another night. Meals, such as salads, can't be frozen and don't keep well. As such, this tip only works for meals that freeze and reheat easily.

Tip #4: Slow-Cooker Dinners

One of my colleagues had a really busy life with her son. Not only did she have him to worry about, but she was working fulltime and going to school part-time as well. So, after a long hard day of work, she would need to care for him, have dinner ready, and be off to school or do homework. When I asked her what her secret was, she said, *"A crockpot."* Apparently, the night before, my colleague would prepare the slow-cooker with all the ingredients and, the following day, dinner was already made when everyone got home. Talk about saving time! After the kids were in bed and her homework completed, she would prepare the slow-cooker for the next day's meal.

My issue with this tip was that I was gone at work roughly 11 hours a day from the time I left to the time I got back. Most recipes for slow-cookers are not intended to cook for 12 hours. Most cook somewhere between 4 and 8 hours. My issue was that my food would either be burned or dried out because it would sit in the heat for too long. So, I upgraded to a slow-cooker that would switch to a "warm" setting after it was done cooking. This, however, still didn't solve the problem. The slow-cooker was just too hot and the food would sit on the "Warm" setting for too long.

Well, someone heard my cry of frustration and solved this little issue. You can now purchase special plugs that connect to your cell phone via Wi-Fi. They are called "Smart Plugs" or "Smart Socket Outlets." You plug this special gadget into your electrical outlet and then plug your slow-cooker into it. When you leave home to go to work or run errands, you can turn on your slow-cooker before leaving home. Set a timer on your cell phone for when the slow-cooker should be turned off. When the timer rings, you can use your phone to turn off the power to your slow-cooker, eliminating burnt or dried-out meals.

Tip #5: Use Crockpot Liners

This is another tip passed down to me by my sister. She is a Crockpot Queen and Crockpot liners are one of her special little helpers! A Crockpot liner is like a plastic bag that goes into your slow-cooker. All the food goes into this plastic bag and you then cook your meal. Once dinner is over, you can either lift the bag out (and any leftovers) into plastic containers to store in the fridge, or simply throw it out. Why is this a tip? Because using the liner means you do not have to scrub the slow-cooker out later. Instead, all you have to do is give your slow-cooker a quick rinse. No need to scrub out crispy, over-cooked food.

Tip #6: Do Not Be Afraid of a Messy House

Most of my girlfriends that have super crazy lifestyles (like two jobs and multiple kids) say that this is a super important tip! Although this tip is not helping you manage anything, they believe it needs to be included, and here is why: *You can't do it all!* No one is super-human, and thus, no one can do it all, all the time. My girlfriends want you to know that a messy house is not a big deal at the end of the day, and that you should not be sacrificing precious time with your kids, or hours of important sleep, to clean up after toys.

Now, there is a difference between "dirty" and "messy." "Dirty" relates more to spilled food on the floor, dirt, and other crud that collects in a house. "Messy" is toys scattered, maybe a pair of shoes out of place, papers on the table, etc. So, when we say "messy," we mean that you should not fuss over clothes, toys, and disorganization in general. Instead, focus your efforts on keeping the house *clean* and not necessarily *organized*. So if the dishes are done, food put away, the cat's litter box is unsoiled, and spills of milk are cleaned up, then relax! Go spend time with your baby, or escape and get in a shower. Having a "messy" house does not make you a failure or a "bad" mom or dad. It makes you human like all the rest of us! The toys will be fine on the floor, the clothes in the hamper can wait for another day, and the decorative pillows on the floor of the family room will survive without your intervention. Like we said, do not be afraid of a messy house.

Tip #7: Do Not Be Afraid of a Crying Baby

This tip actually came from my husband, who has had his moments of caring for Rachel too. When I asked him what he thought would be important for you to hear, this was it. Surprisingly, some of my girlfriends also agreed.

Biologically and psychologically speaking, we *hate* hearing a baby or toddler cry. You could say it's nature's way of making sure we provide our children with what they need to ensure their survival. Hearing a baby cry sends chills down our backs and is right up there with nails on a chalkboard. This is why my husband thought it should be included as a tip.

Just like Tip #6, this one does not help you manage anything, but it is important for you to know. Letting your baby or toddler cry for a few minutes in a swing will not hurt him! If you have to go to the restroom, or you need to finish chopping a few veggies to add them to the casserole, the baby will live. I know it is absolutely awful to hear that little person cry for you, but he will be fine and he will still love you! I promise. Even if he is hungry or he needs a diaper change, get whatever it is you were working on done, and then attend to him.

Now, do not misunderstand me; I am not saying you should "abandon" your kid so you can have a glass of wine. But, if you are right in the middle of getting some water in a pot to boil noodles when your baby cries, then go ahead and finish putting the noodles on the stove, then go check in on him. If he is safe and crying just to be held, then let him sit in his swing while you finish dinner. You will be able to give him more of your positive attention if you know dinner is baking in the oven and you have a 30 minute break than you would if you stop everything just to soothe him and then try to get back to cooking. I have done the latter, and it turns into you being annoyed with your baby because you can't get dinner going and "all he does is cry!" So, let him cry for a few minutes while you try to finish things up. That way, you will be able to love on him in peace rather than haphazardly rock him so he will hush. You will feel better with less stress, and so will he.

Along this same note, I think it is important to provide

you with some quick tips I give parents in therapy to manage these situations. From a young age, kids seem to know when you are really busy, and that is unsurprisingly the exact moment that they want your complete and undivided attention! A lot of parents I have worked with in the past drop what they are doing and attend to their child, much like discussed here. When I encourage this tip with these parents, they are always concerned their children will feel unloved and abandoned. Here is how you remedy this problem: You acknowledge your child while you make them wait. To explain this better, I will give you an example from my own life.

It was very common for Rachel to completely ignore me while I sat on the floor and played with her, but the second I stood up and started cooking in the kitchen, all of the sudden, she needed my attention. She would tug on my pant leg, try to push me away from the stove, cry and whine, and even start playing with things she knew would get her in trouble. I would not stop what I was doing. I would keep cooking and move around her as long as she was not in danger of hurting herself. While I worked around her, I would talk to her, saying things like, *"I know you are upset right now. I am sorry, but Mommy needs to make dinner so we can eat. Mommy will play with you when she is done."* If she cried, I would add something to the effect of, *"I am sorry you are mad right now. Mommy sees you and I hear you. I am not ignoring you. I love you and I will hold you in a few minutes."*

I began saying these things to her the second I brought her home from the hospital. By doing this, you are showing your child that their feelings are important and being heard. This keeps your child from feeling "abandoned." You might be thinking that babies do not understand what we are saying, so how can this possibly help? I will assure you that our children understand far more than we give them credit for; they just can't articulate their understanding yet. So, I encourage you to try this!

I had a client of mine try this with her 7 year old son who suffered from Attention Deficit, Hyper-Activity Disorder (ADHD). She found that doing this small gesture decreased her child's meltdowns in the afternoon by half! Feeling acknowledged by his mother was all this boy needed, even if she did not stop everything to attend to him. So, try it out… you have nothing to lose and everything to gain!

Tip #8: Find a Routine & Stick with It

This tip is my own advice to you. I found that home-life ran much smoother when I knew exactly what I needed to do and in what order I needed to do it in. It also meant less arguing with my husband because there was an understanding of whose job it was to do each task.

For us, whoever came home first was responsible for getting dinner started (usually me). Whoever came home second was responsible for watching Rachel (usually Dave). While I cooked, Dave got to spend quality time with her, playing and dancing to music. Once dinner was made, Dave would begin eating while I settled Rachel in her chair for dinner. I would then feed her while taking the occasional bite of my own meal. After Dave finished eating, he would finish feeding Rachel while I finished my own food. Typically, this would be over by 7:15ish. I would then spend quality time with Rachel until 7:30ish when it was bath time. Now, David hated doing dishes, so he would bathe her while I cleaned up the kitchen. When bath time was done (about 8:00ish), I would feed Rachel a bottle and rock her to sleep. This was our routine. It was not perfect, but it worked at keeping us going every day.

Now, you might be thinking to yourself, *"Hey, what about laundry and other chores?"* Well, for us, we would leave Sunday for cleaning house in the morning (especially while Rachel napped), and then tried doing fun activities together in the afternoon. By getting the cleaning done on the weekends, it meant I could just focus on dinner, baths, and playtime during the week. This took a lot of stress off of me, and helped me stay calm during busy weeks.

There were times in my life when my husband would travel on business, which meant that my routine would shift in order to manage it all by myself. I was lucky because David only traveled for five days at a time on average. So I did not have to manage the extra work on my own for too long, but this is a reality for many couples, or simply for the single-parent. Sometimes you have to manage all of these tasks on your own. You will find that a routine will really help with this situation.

Tip #9: Wear Your Baby Everywhere!

After speaking to several different moms, this was a tip that came up over and over again. When I was pregnant with Rachel, I had heard about "Baby Wearing," and was intrigued with the concept. My sister-in-law swore by this, and she insisted I buy a Moby Wrap. There are a lot of slings, wraps, and carriers out there, and they all have their pros and cons, but wearing your baby is definitely a life-saver!

If you are not familiar with the concept of Baby Wearing, it is basically wearing your baby in a fabric or some sort of carrier that keeps the baby close to your body while keeping your hands free to do whatever it is you need to get done! For the busy mom, this is a great and amazing thing. As you might remember, Rachel was always crying in those early months, and I could never put her down. My little girl would never go down for naps either, which made it extremely hard to get anything done in my house. This is when I started using a baby carrier (the one I used was called a Moby Wrap).

Rachel absolutely loved being in the Moby Wrap and frequently would nap for hours in it. I am not exaggerating. The first time I placed her in the wrap, she made a little bit of a fuss, but after walking around for five minutes, she settled right in and fell asleep. It was a miracle for me! My baby was finally sleeping, and I could still use my hands! I would fold laundry, do dishes (a little difficult with her right in front of me, but manageable), eat breakfast/lunch/dinner, etc. I have one girlfriend that would even vacuum while wearing her munchkin! It is amazing what you can get done around the house while wearing your baby. My sister-in-law would wrap herself in her Moby before getting in the car, drive to the market, stick her baby in the Moby while in the parking lot, and then get her grocery shopping done in peace!

Baby Wearing is also very helpful with multiples. When you have a little toddler running around and a new baby, you need your hands free as much as possible for your tot! Wearing the baby allows you to keep your infant close to you while also being able to manage your other child! Refreshing, right?

There are many types, styles, and brands of baby carriers out there. Unfortunately, all of these carriers can be a little on the pricy side, so I would consider adding them to your Baby Registry. If that is not an option, consider asking fellow family members if they have one you can use as a hand-me-down, or check out thrift shops or online stores (like Amazon) for used ones. My sister-in-law found a free pattern online on how to sew a baby carrier known as a Mei Tai, which I also adored! She made it for me as a gift when I had my little one. If you, or someone you know, is crafty with a needle, you can always try making your own!

Tip #10: Create a Family Calendar

As your Little One gets older and starts to get involved in community –based activities, like Baby Ballet classes or Mommy-and-Me swim lessons, you'll find that remembering everything starts to become challenging. Then, if your spouse is involved in their own extracurricular activities, like going to the gym or volunteering with a local church, things become even harder to keep track of. The answer is a Family Calendar. A Family Calendar is one primary calendar that everyone in the family contributes to and has access to. Everyone takes part in inputting events, dates-to-remember, or re-occurring activities, like piano lessons for example. The calendar needs to be easily accessed by everyone, such as on the fridge. This makes it easy for everybody to add to it and keep track of the different events. There are tons of ways to do this too, it's just a matter of what works best for you and your family.

For my husband and I, we have an online, shared Google calendar. Everything is color coordinated, and everything goes into the calendar. Anything my husband adds is in red. Anything that has to do with Rachel is in pink, and everything for me is in purple. Doctor's appointments, holidays, ballet lessons, nights that I work late, days Dave plays golf with friends, daycare closure days, etc., gets added into the calendar. Then, I have the calendar synced to my phone, which means I can check the calendar from anywhere! So when someone asks me if I can volunteer for X event, I pull out my phone and check our Family Calendar. If I'm clear, I add the event to the calendar.

Another way of having a Family Calendar is one of those giant desktop calendars that you hang in a central place in your home, like the kitchen. Everyone can write (in pencil!) the different events that need to be remembered. You can also try one of those dry-erase board calendars too!

Some people have a hard time remembering to add things to the calendar. One way to help remedy this is to set a day every week where items are added to the calendar in a collaborative effort. For example, I advised one family to have a Family Meeting every Sunday. On that day, everyone would report to Mom all of the events going on that they had become aware of. This included birthday parties, recitals, sports practices, and even big school projects that were going to require parental time and resources. This helped the family to keep all the important dates in mind, and it allowed Mom and Dad to help remind the kids about those school projects and keep tabs on the child's progress with those assignments.

For the very busy parent, a Family Calendar can really help organize you and your family. It will help minimize stress by making sure important items aren't forgotten or remembered last minute, and really helps you and your partner to communicate.

Tip #11: Host Family Meetings

Alright, so I already kind of gave this one away. Tip #11 is to schedule Family Meetings. Like I mentioned previously, I typically recommend it weekly, but I know some folks who like to do it daily and some who do it monthly. Usually, weekly is a pretty safe way to go, especially if you have multiple kids or older children who are involved in a lot of extracurricular activities. Family Meetings give everyone in the family the opportunity to share dates or upcoming events that are important to them. It guarantees everyone a time and place to be able to speak and share with you what's going on in their lives. This can be a formal meeting where everyone sits down at a scheduled time every Sunday, but it doesn't have to be. For families who are constantly on-the-go, having the meeting over dinner on Friday night works just as well! You or your partner can be in charge of writing the information on the Family Calendar while everyone is eating. This gives you a meal that you all get to share together while you get to discuss different items that are important to your spouse and children, AND it doesn't take up any *extra* time to do!

It doesn't really matter how you host Family

Meetings, but they can be a great asset to you at keeping organized and managing home-life, especially if you have multiple kiddos to keep tabs on!

Dealing with Home-Life as a Single Parent

Although I am not a single-mom raising a kid, I did experience what it was like to be a single-parent when my husband traveled. I must say, my hat goes off to the moms and dads who do this every single day!

I spoke to a few friends and clients of mine who are single-parents, and the primary advice they gave me was to FIND HELP! For most of them, they relied heavily on friends and family to fill in the gaps that they could not do themselves. Many were on tight budgets, so hiring help or paying for daycare was not much of an option. Most had grandparents or aunts/uncles who were willing to babysit or watch the baby while they cleaned house or ran errands. But at some point, they came home to an empty house and had to fend for themselves with their kids.

When Dave traveled for work, I remember I would get up extra early so that I could get dressed, make my lunch for the day, and have Rachel's diaper bag packed and ready with everything she needed for her day at daycare or grandma's house. By getting up an hour earlier, I was all ready to go by the time she woke up. That means that all I had to focus on was getting her dressed and fed. This made mornings run smoothly, though a little sleepy. I would drive her to daycare or grandma's (which was the opposite direction of my job), and then went to work, sipping coffee on the way. When I picked her up, I would bring her home, and have dinner, baths, and the bedtime routine as usual. Once she was asleep, I enjoyed my own dinner, bath, and would go right to bed.

During these times, I would highly rely on slow-cooker and easy meals, like spaghetti, so that cooking was minimal or already done. I would not worry too much about dishes except for loading them in the dishwasher. Believe it or not, this whole process would run so smoothly, I was usually in bed by 9:00 in the evening (earlier than nights when Dave was around!). So, I was typically pretty rested when 5:00 in the morning came to call on me.

Speaking with single-parents out there, I asked them what they thought about the tips listed previously, and for the most part, they all agreed that these tips helped them manage single-parenthood as well. The most important tip, they reported, was keeping a routine. Children love to know what is happening in their lives and thrive on structure. Having a schedule for your home is an easy way to increase compliance from those troublesome toddlers and make life easier on you too!

7. QUALITY TIME IS FAMILY TIME

At some point in your day, you want to make room to spend time with your child. As a therapist, I usually recommend at least one hour of time dedicated to each kid. That is in addition to time you already spend with your kids as a group or whole family (i.e. all kids together at one time). That can be A LOT if you have three or more kids and are trying to manage a job and home-life. Our kids want our attention, and they want us to be a part of their lives. Children will frequently misbehave when they feel like their parents are not spending enough time with them because they would rather have negative attention (i.e. Mommy yelling because they poked Tommy) than no attention at all. This fact baffles the parents I work with, but I assure you that it is true.

One hour a day per child (i.e. 3 kids means 3 hours) can consume a lot of time, and parents will often fail to do this because they have a mountain of other chores to accomplish. I was one of those parents too! Do not feel bad. I suspect most parents fail to give their kids this one hour of undivided attention. And, a lot of times, parents think that forcing their kids to do something with them (the parents) that the kids do not want to do, counts towards the one hour… it doesn't. So, let us talk about quality time with your kids and work on figuring out ways for you to incorporate it into your already busy schedule.

Defining Quality Time

To place a rigid definition of "quality time" would be silly, because "quality time" is different for every person and every family. For me as a therapist, it is essentially spending time engaging in an activity that the other person enjoys. For example, quality time for me might be soaking in a spa tub, snoozing away an afternoon. But, you better believe that it is not quality time for Rachel. My little girl would much rather go down the slide 100 times in a row than watch me sleep in a tub.

The same concept above applies for dads and the TV. I remember one day I asked Dave to spend some quality time with Rachel. He happily picked her up and turned on the football game while holding her in his lap. She, of course, got bored after a minute and slid off his lap to play by herself with blocks on the floor. When I walked into the room and found her playing, I asked him why he was not spending time with her. He replied, *"I am! We are watching the game together."* He was dead serious…. Much like the bathtub example, this is *not* "quality time."

So, when we talk about "quality time" in this chapter, we should really be thinking of time spent with your child in an activity of *his* or *her* choosing. Once you think of "quality time" as <u>engaging</u> in something <u>your child enjoys</u> and not simply being in the same room as your kid, conceptualizing "quality time" becomes easier. Not only does it become easier to conceptualize, but it also becomes easier to figure out what counts and what does not. Finally, once you know what counts and what doesn't, you will be able to figure out how to squeeze in that one hour of quality time a lot easier!

Engaging in Quality Time during the Week

Rachel enjoyed many things as a toddler. She loved playing in the bathtub, loved swimming, loved to dance to music, and loved watching cartoons and cuddling in the morning. All four of these items became instant ways of sharing in quality time with one another. Early in the morning, before Dave took her to daycare, I would cuddle with her while she drank milk and watched Mickey Mouse cartoons. In the afternoons over the summer, she had infant swim lessons, and Dave would jump in the pool with her to teach her how to swim. Once at home, Dave and her would dance to music in the family room while I made dinner. Then, I would feed her at the dinner table while telling her stories and asking her questions about her day. Baths were done by Dave mostly, or myself if needed, and the bedtime routine of cuddling and being rocked to sleep or read to was done by me. All of these different activities being listed above counted towards quality time. Each thing listed was something that Rachel wanted and loved to do. (It was super lucky for us that she enjoyed activities that needed to get done anyways!) That is why it counted as "quality time." And if you add up how much time we spent with her doing each item, I'm sure Dave and I would both have met our daily quota of at least one hour.

The primary thing to realize is that one hour does not have to be in one sitting. It can be divided up throughout the day with several different activities. The important thing is that you engage with your child in some way that is meaningful to him or her. If your son loves watching football, then Dad lucks out and watching football on the couch counts! The primary point is that the activity is something that your child enjoys.

As a working parent, it is ok if you strategize and use your awesome time management skills to make this all work! My dad used to take me on errands with him as a way to spend time with me. That totally counted! He would play games with me in the car, like "I Spy," and tell me made-up stories about bears and princesses, all while getting his errands to the bank and the store done. The "errand running" part does not count towards the one hour, but the fact that he incorporated a chore like this, with storytelling and games is what makes this viable "quality time."

Another example comes from my mom. My little sister loved completing puzzles, so my mom would watch her favorite TV show while doing puzzles with my little sister on the floor. Again, the TV show part does not count, but the puzzle solving does!

A great resource to check out is The Family Dinner Project. They have a website (see Bibliography) that is all about families sharing meals together. In an effort to make family meals more appealing to kids and parents, they have several articles that give great ideas on how to make a meal at the dinner table something your whole family will love and cherish! Check out some of their suggestions and give them a try. You just might find that your child starts to love dinner time because they get to spend quality time with you!

So, what's the main point of this section? Get creative! Find some activities you can do while enjoying time with your child. Just do your best to spend lots of time with your children. The more time you spend, the better it is for you and them!

Engaging in Quality Time on the Weekend

Weekends are an amazing thing, and they sure do help us keep it together during the work week when things get tough. Although you try your hardest and get as creative as you possibly can, you may discover that you just can't squeeze in enough time with your baby. If this is your situation, then rest assured that all is not lost! There were many weeks while raising Rachel where I was barely keeping it together. My work seemed to follow me home and time flew by. And, even though Dave was giving her *his* time, she was not getting that special bonding time with *me*. Weekends, however, were a completely different story. Weekends provided me with an opportunity to be the engaging, awesome, super mom I always thought I would be, and that helped me feel more competent as a mother too.

When Rachel was about 10 months old, my husband and I bought our first home, and it was one heck of a fixer-upper! Dave ended up spending many of our weekends working on the new house to help us save money while I stayed home with the baby. As hard as these moments were because I needed to get all the cleaning and organizing done, they were also very rewarding. Many cuddles, hugs, kisses, laughs, naps, playing, exploring, talking/babbling were had between my baby and I on those weekends. Even though I could not always give Rachel my undivided attention during the week, I know I made up for a lot of it by being her biggest fan and follower on the weekends.

As Rachel got older, she became more curious on how the world works; she even wanted to conduct "experiments." This spurred a whole new world of quality time for my family. My husband started looking for little science projects he could conduct with Rachel on the weekends. This slowly became a family tradition; every other weekend, they would conduct a science experiment together. They did everything from making elephant toothpaste, to making tie dye t-shirts. A great resource I found while shopping one day was *The 101 Simple Science Experiments: Awesome Things To Do With Your Parents, Babysitters and Other Adults* by Holly Homer, Rachel Miller, and Jamie Harrington. It's a book jam-packed with science projects to do with your kids. Rachel loves flipping through the pages and looking for the next experiment she wants to complete with her dad. I also discovered another book by Holly Homer and Rachel Miller entitled *101 Kids Activities That Are the Bestest, Funniest Ever!: The Entertainment Solution for Parents, Relatives & Babysitters.* I highly recommend them if you are desperate for ideas on how to spend some fun time with your little ones!

WARNING! Don't Be This Parent...!

I have had parents in the past interpret information from this chapter as saying that they can completely ignore their child during the week and make up for it by taking them to a theme park on Saturday. That is not how it works. Your child deserves your time and attention each and every day of the week. If you have time to play a video game when you get home from work, then you have time to cuddle your baby or watch a family movie with your toddler. Parenting takes place 24 hours a day, 365 days a year. Ignoring your child so that you can snooze, play your computer game, or watch your TV show is not what is best for your child. Many of the children I work with have behavioral issues, not because they have a mental health condition, but because they are starved for parental attention. Please spend time with your son or daughter.

Now, if you come home and barely have time to eat and take a shower, that is different. You might need to put the quality time on hold to address your basic needs, but we will talk more about that in a little bit. What I am addressing is the parent who comes home, eats, and then sits down and reads a magazine (plays a video game, takes a nap, etc...) while the other parent cooks, cleans, and tries to watch the kids. This is an unhappy scenario, and I strongly urge you to reconsider how you manage home-life. If this is your situation, consider seeing a Family Therapist who can assist you in creating a better home environment for you and your family.

When Time Is Not Enough

I am aware that there are times when so much is piled upon us that we never get around to quality time with our kids. Let me be the first to tell you that it is *ok!* Not being able to fit in some quality time does not make you a bad parent! It means you are stuck in a situation that is keeping you from being the parent that you want to be. I know exactly how you feel, and I wish I had the guts to tell someone how I felt when this happened to me, but I did not. I carried this horrible sense of guilt around within me because I felt I was missing out on Rachel's precious toddler years! I was not being the mom I had always envisioned I would be, and I felt like a terrible, failing parent. Many times, I questioned having a second child because I felt I barely had enough time for the first one. It took me a long time to finally cut myself some slack and accept that I was not a horrible mother. In fact, I was a good one. I was just stuck in a financial situation that required my husband and I to both work fulltime.

Having these thoughts and realizations allowed me to appreciate and understand my own parents. I realized my mother was extremely lucky to be able to work from home, and my father was a selfless person who gave up his involvement in our childhood as a sacrifice so we could have a mother who could stay home with us. These revelations also allowed me to realize one more thing... I loved my parents and they were both great parents. If my dad was not able to give us all that quality time that experts talk about, and *he* was *still* a good dad, a dad who I loved very much, then that meant that Rachel still loved me, and *I* was not a bad mom.

You are not a bad mom. You are not a bad dad. You are a parent who is trying your very best to meet your children's physical and emotional needs. Sometimes our life circumstances are far from perfect, but it does not mean that we can't be good parents. Your child deserves your time, and you deserve time with your child. So, get creative! Tell those stories while driving to the market, or do a puzzle while watching TV, or play "I Spy" with your kid while you cook dinner, or simply cuddle him a little longer when putting him to sleep at night. Find little tricks to share special moments with your children that allow you to still manage your job and home-life while letting your child feel loved and cared for. You both deserve quality time together. The little time you manage to squeeze in will remain in their memories for a lifetime! So, be gentle on yourself, try your best, and remember, they will still love you at the end of the day.

If you want more great ideas on how to incorporate more quality time with your kids into your tight schedule, you can check out my blog post, *Tips for Quality Time with Your Kids without Adding to Your Plate!* You can find it at:

www.kcdreisbach.com/single-post/Quality-Time-with-Your-Kids

8. TO SCHEDULE OR NOT TO SCHEDULE...?

Just about every baby or toddler book out there talks about placing your child on a schedule. But then, you might have friends that tell you a schedule is a super bad idea. I know that was my situation. One part of my family was all about schedules while another part of my family believed schedules were useless. The reality is that it really depends on your child. Some kids really need a schedule... they just do immensely better with one. One of my girlfriends was able to get her 4 month old sleeping all through the night (with the exception of teething/illness), and she swears that it was because she placed her little girl on a schedule from day one! I have another friend who hated schedules, and who told me over and over again that your child will sleep through the night sooner if you do not have them on a schedule, as was the case with her child. These two examples are exact opposites, and they both had babies who started sleeping through the night very early on. So what gives?

79

Why Schedules Work & Why They Don't

Schedules can be very advantageous to you and your children. Research has often found that children thrive best when they know what to expect. That is one of the reasons why bedtime routines help your children fall asleep, because they know the course of events and what is expected to happen at any given point. A routine and structure helps children know what is happening next in their lives, and thus, helps reduce the chance of a tantrum or meltdowns. It also helps you map out your day and provides you with the motivation to stay on task and not give in to little pleas for "just a few more minutes."

Not all children, however, do well on schedules. Some kids have a difficult time adapting to routines that are completely against their natural rhythm. For example, if your child normally gets sleepy at eight o'clock in the evening, but you are forcing them to go to sleep at seven o' clock at night, you are going to have a problem. Like adults, children have a natural body rhythm and not all their body rhythms are the same. Forcing your baby to fit into the mold of a schedule that is against his natural rhythm is going to give you quite the headache. Knowing this information, what do you do? The answer is simply trial and error.

Since research shows that children do better with a routine or structure in general, then it is in your best interest to provide that to them. We know, however, that a schedule that goes against their natural body rhythm will only distress you and them. The key is to design a routine that flows with your child's natural instincts. But how do you do that? This is the tricky part.

The simplest way is to observe your child for a week and take notes. For example, when Rachel was a year old, she still wasn't sleeping through the night like so many of her peers. I gave in at one point and hired a sleep consultant. I must admit, the consultant did help us improve Rachel's sleep tremendously, as well as gave me moral support to make it through every night, but at 1 ½ years of age, Rachel was still getting up about once a night (about two o' clock in the morning) and ended up in our bed. Our consultant insisted that the reason why Rachel was not sleeping all the way through the night was because she was not going to bed until about 8:30 p.m. The consultant stated that, based on Rachel's schedule, she should be asleep by 6:30 p.m. Yeah right! I got home from work at 6:30 p.m., how was I expected to have her asleep by that time?

Regardless of the unrealistic expectations, I tried my very best to get her to sleep earlier. You know what I found? No matter how early she went to bed, or how perfect her bedtime routine was, or how consistent I was about it, or how much exercise she got during the day, or how well she napped, Rachel would not go to sleep any earlier. The couple of times I did manage to get her to sleep at seven o'clock in the evening, she still woke up at two in the morning, or she would sleep even worse! Thus, Rachel's natural body rhythm was to be asleep between eight-thirty and nine o'clock in the evening. Moreover, I had some nights where Rachel slept right through! And guess what? She went to bed at eight-thirty each time and not any earlier! So, through trial and error, I learned that fighting with her to go to sleep earlier, at a time that was against her natural body rhythm, was a useless and tiresome battle.

Another reason why schedules work for some kids and not others has to do with the child's temperament. Some kids are very easy and go with the flow. They nap wherever, eat whatever, and, in general, are low maintenance children. They are fairly low energy kids, and they do just fine with no schedule or very little routine. These kids are often referred to as "good babies" or "angel babies." Some kids, however, are a little more cautious or anxious, and need those cues to tell them it's time to eat, play, or sleep. These kids also tend to be a little more adventurous and have more energy. I have heard these children referred to as "colicky babies" or "spirited." These kiddos do better with much more structure. Then, you have a mass of children who fall in between, which is what most parents encounter.

Rachel was an "in between" toddler. She was high energy and cautious, but also fairly mellow with mild tantrums, but sometimes needy. She was pretty good about napping anywhere (like grandma's house or at a party), but if she wasn't in her highchair for meals, she wouldn't eat. Essentially, she required cues for some activities (like eating) but no cues for other things (like napping). The result was a baby who needed a momma that wasn't rigid in a schedule, but still provided some outline of a routine for her day. So, I had a basic sequence of events or activities that we would follow for the day, and rough time estimates of when I wanted these activities completed. None of these activities, however, were set in stone, and would be adjusted as needed to suit Rachel's needs.

Baby Schedules & the Working Parent

After figuring out that Rachel didn't function well without some sort of routine to help guide her throughout the day, I attempted to create a schedule for her, as mentioned previously. I worked hard at it, making notes of her habits on the weekends, and logging her sleep during the day and night. I read several baby books that had examples on how to create routines and schedules for toddlers/babies, and I did my best to replicate them. I typed it out, emailed it to my parents and my husband, and stuck to it as religiously as I could on the weekends. You know what happened? It didn't work.

If you recall the chapter on childcare, I talk about the pros and cons of the different childcare options for the working parent. One of the cons I listed for caregivers was that you really cannot force your idea of the schedule your baby should be on. And that's exactly the problem I encountered. Despite my parents' great efforts to match the schedule I created, their own daily plans often didn't match up with the schedule I labored over. Rachel napped best in a home with a bed or crib (didn't matter where the bed was), not in a car-seat. Even as an infant, the car was great for getting her to fall asleep, but terrible at keeping her asleep. Rachel would come home cranky and tired, and I couldn't get her to sleep when I needed her to at night. After some investigation, I found out that my parents were running errands during her nap time, which meant Rachel had to sleep in her car-seat in between stops. This translated into a kid who was overtired at night because of naps that were too short and constantly interrupted during the day. What was I to do?

Other examples were when Rachel stayed with my in-laws. Even though she would nap in their home (not on the road), she was often put down for naps too late in the afternoon. This caused problems for Dave and I because Rachel wouldn't be sleepy until way past ten in the evening. This meant that I was up late with her at night, and I would be one very tired (and cranky) momma in the morning at work.

Sorry to tell you, you can't force schedules on your child's caregivers. And even if you tried, it's unfair to expect them to match your needs when they are already doing you a favor. I don't blame my parents or in-laws for these dilemmas. Quite simply, the problem is a classic one for working parents, and a big reason why I thought it important to discuss it here.

The reality is that schedules during the week may not happen, at least not the way you intend them to. All you can do is try your best to create some semblance of a routine for your child. When they are home with you in the evening or on the weekend, do your best to provide them with the structure they need. Kids are very intelligent and, over time, they begin to figure out what rules exist for each environment they are in. (This is why kids will be great at school but tyrants at home.) Your toddler will eventually figure out that, at grandma's, we do "A," and at daddy's house we do "B," and at daycare we do "C." In the beginning, it will be rough, especially when they are under the age of one, but eventually, they figure out the different sets of rules. Just keep doing your routine, and your baby will eventually fall right in sync.

"If You Can't Beat Them, Join Them!"

As a parent, it is really frustrating when you have little control over your child's day. When you can't give your child the structure you want, it can be exasperating and upsetting. Trust me, I was there and completely understand. During one of my moments of frustration, I accepted that, during the week, I was going to have very little (if any) control over Rachel's life. I could control the few hours in the evening and the weekends, but the majority of her life and development was in the hands of the caregivers I had placed in charge. And that is when it struck me… that even though I couldn't control her caregivers, I did have control over myself.

There's the old saying that goes, "If you can't beat them, join them!" If you can't force your caregiver or daycare to place your child on the routine you want for him/her, your next option would be to change your routine. In this case, I am suggesting you change your schedule for the one your child has to follow while you're at work. For example, if at grandpa's, Little Billy has lunch at one o'clock instead of at 12 p.m., then you can change your weekend routine to reflect one o'clock as lunch time. The same thing goes for play time, nap time, when baths happen, etc. The key is to follow a routine that is similar to your caregiver's. That way, your baby gets the same schedule every day of the week.

I want to note that this suggestion may not be feasible for you because your household's needs might be different than your caregiver's. If you find, however, that your child's weekday schedule is doable for you, *and* you are in approval of the activities and the sequence of events, then why not just give it a try and see how it goes? The worst case scenario is that it doesn't work well and you go back to your previous way of doing things. It doesn't hurt to try it out. You have nothing to lose and everything to gain! Who knows, the new schedule might be a nice change of pace. Like I said, it's just another idea to help you out on your journey.

9. MANAGING YOUR CHILD'S SLEEP HABITS

Sleep was one of the most difficult things to manage while raising Rachel. She had a love-hate relationship with it really, like a lot of kids do. And for Rachel, her difficulties started straight off in the hospital from birth. I remember that first night she was up every hour wanting to eat, and I would nurse her for about 1 ½ hours each time. The lactation consultant at the hospital said she was "cluster feeding." When she wasn't nursing, she needed to be held. In fact, the few times the nurses wrapped her up and tried putting her in the bassinet failed miserably! She would remain quiet for a few minutes before erupting in explosive anger and tears. Later on, they figured out that she was jaundice and that my milk supply was very low because of my anemia. I'm not sure if the hunger in the hospital set the stage for her poor sleep, or if it was simply an omen to me that Rachel would be a challenge for bedtime and naps. All I know is that my biggest trials were between me, Rachel, and the crib.

Rachel's Sleep History

As mentioned, nighttime sleep was always a challenge for my baby girl. She started off in a bassinet in our master bedroom since I breastfed her at night. In all honesty, she slept ok in this bassinet once she was a month old. The first few weeks of her life, however, were much more difficult. She would wake for long hours at night, crying and fussing with no end in sight. My mother-in-law and my mom helped me out a lot by staying with me some nights to watch the baby so Dave and I could get some rest. But once they went home, it was all me.

I remember those nights and I remember how lonely it felt, bouncing a crying baby back and forth from room to room. I remember crying a lot too, riding those crashing waves of hormones while begging my infant to hush. I hated the clock… every minute ticking by was a personal assault against one of the things I treasured the most… sleep. And she just kept crying, and crying, and crying…. One of those nights, I put her in her crib, needing a break very badly. Listening to her scream in anguish, however, hurt my heart so much that I picked her right back up. It was my own personal hell, a crying baby that I could do nothing about.

Those nights were so miserable, and I remember people telling me that it ends and that I would forget my misery. They told me that once I forgot my misery, I would want another sweet bouncing baby… and that was a terrifying thought. I remember cradling Rachel as she sobbed and speaking to myself, *"Don't you forget this Krystal.*

Don't you forget how awful this is!" (Please don't misunderstand me. I loved and still love my daughter with all my heart, and if I had to do it again, I most certainly would. I have no regrets!)

Eventually, Rachel started sleeping better, giving me nice long stretches at night where she didn't sob and actually slept. It wasn't until she was about 2 months old that Rachel slept through the night for the first time. I was so happy that night. She slept from eight o' clock until seven the next day. It was a blessing. I remember taking her to her doctor's appointment and him telling me to wake her up during those long stretches to feed. (Yeah right! Was he nuts? I needed to sleep!) Besides, Rachel was a very big girl, and in the 90th percentile for height and weight. There was no way I was going to wake her up to feed, and I didn't. She slept like this for two months until she did not sleep anymore. And that's when the *real* hell began.

From 4 months of age and on, Rachel struggled to sleep. She cried and screamed if she wasn't snuggled in my arms. For a period of time, we tried co-sleeping, but the issue was that she moved a lot in her sleep. I was constantly being poked in the eye and punched in the face, which made for very poor sleep for me. To make matters worse, Rachel would wake up around four o'clock in the morning and proceeded to jump on my stomach. And the more I pulled her down, the funnier she thought it was. And I could not just let her do it because it hurt, not to mention that I had to get up and function at a job the next day.

Eventually, I became desperate enough that I

attempted to let her cry-it-out, but those sobs were just too much to bear. And being a therapist, I worried about attachment and abandonment issues. We quickly gave this up, and graduated to more "professional" methods when Rachel was about a year old. I paid for a sleep consultation service, and it resulted in being a great idea and help! The service included a 30 page, step-by-step plan of how to get my little one sleeping through the night without leaving her to cry. We stuck to this plan confidently and consistently, and ended up with great results.

At some point, teething became an additional barrier to sleep, and reversed a lot of the success we had previously experienced with our sleep consultations. Dave hated sleep training and really didn't want to go back to any of it regardless of how well it worked. Eventually, Rachel graduated to a "Big Girl Bed" when she was 1 ½ years old, and although the sleep trouble didn't end here, they got a lot better.

Helping Your Child Sleep: Tips to Manage Home-Life at Bedtime

I'm not a sleep expert… let me just start off by making that clear. But in my journey of raising Rachel, I have become quite educated on the topic, and I have discussed it with many experts and mommas alike. I don't want to delve too much into this topic because there are many great books on the subject and some awesome, free blogs you can read on the internet. But in my effort to provide you a book to help you manage your life as a fulltime parent and fulltime career-person, I thought it appropriate to discuss it at least a little bit. As such, I collected the following tips to help you manage your child's bedtime and nighttime-wakings.

Tip #1: Develop a Bedtime Routine & Be Consistent with It

Bedtime routines are singularly the most popular tip you will read in just about any childrearing book on the market, and it most certainly plays an important role in your baby or toddler's sleep. There are plenty of internet blogs that will give you examples of bedtime routines for free and will explain them in great detail. So, I'm not going to do that here. What I *will* do here is let you know that it is totally OK if your bedtime routine starts and/or ends later than the average recommendation on the internet. Allow me to explain....

As I read book after book on baby sleep, I consistently saw the recommendation that Rachel should be put to sleep at 6:30 in the evening. Previously in this text, I mentioned that I frequently did not get home from work until 6:30 p.m. How was I going to have her in bed at that same hour? When I spoke to the sleep consultants, they kept insisting on a six o'clock bedtime, and when I mentioned my job, they did not provide any solutions.

So, what I'm saying is that it is OK if you can't have your baby in bed until nine o'clock at night. You guys will work it out. Just try your best to get Junior tucked in as early as you can, but if it is later than the popular recommendation of six in the evening, you and your child will be just fine.

The most important part of this tip is that you start the bedtime routine roughly around the same time every day and end it roughly around the same time every day, whatever that time is. Next, do your best to keep it going every day of the week (including weekends, which is totally hard!). All activities in the bedtime routine should be things your child enjoys (i.e. do not make baths part of the mix if your kid hates baths), and finally, try your best to keep it low- key and simple. All of these components make for a good bedtime routine. Here is an example:

<u>Rachel's Bedtime Routine</u>
8:15 p.m. – Bath
8: 30 p.m. – Bottle and Cuddle
8:40 p.m. – Tucked in Bed
8:45 p.m. – Story Time
9:00 p.m. – Lights Out

As you can see, Rachel's bedtime routine lasted about 45 minutes, with some nights a little less and others a little longer. Many books recommend a much shorter bedtime routine, closer to 15 or 25 minutes at the most. The short routines did not work for Rachel, and she was never sleepy at the end of them. This routine was long enough to have her drowsy when the lights went out. Also, plenty of baby book authors would be horrified at the late bedtime (9:00 p.m.! Yikes!) But given my work schedule and Rachel's temperament, early bedtimes didn't produce any difference in helping her sleep. Furthermore, early bedtimes meant Rachel spent more time crying and avoiding bedtime, and it also meant I got to spend very little quality time with her when I came home. This is the schedule that worked for us, kept me and David sane, and gave us a happy Rachel who actually enjoyed going to sleep in her bed.

The main point I want you to grasp is that a bedtime routine is a good idea, and do not freak out if it is different from all the ones recommended in other baby books that are out there. If your baby is healthy and happy, and you are healthy and happy, then do not stress and just enjoy bedtime. The minute I adopted this point of view, was the minute Rachel no longer battled me to go to sleep… and then I didn't dread bedtime anymore.

Tip #2: Make Sure Your Tot Has a Full Tummy

This was probably one of the most recommended tips from other mommas and daddys out there. Babies and toddlers are burning tons of energy growing and developing, and a hungry tummy can be the culprit to bedtime struggles and nighttime-wakings. This tip is as easy as it sounds; provide a little snack before bedtime to ensure your child has some extra fuel to hold them over until morning. Rachel would usually have a bottle of milk before bedtime (usually a full 8oz bottle), and this kept her nice and full all night long.

You can also provide other snacks like wholegrain crackers, cheese, yogurt, or cheerios. Just avoid sugary stuff like juice, cookies, and candy. These snacks can actually give them a sugar rush and cause a whole new problem for you!

It should go without saying that a baby or a young toddler really should not be consuming caffeine, like soda, tea, and coffee. But if your little tyke is having these beverages, try to avoid them several hours before bedtime.

Tip #3: Avoid Bad Sleep-Associations

Can I start off by saying that I hate sleep-associations! Sleep-associations are things your child associates with sleep, and thus, will make them sleepy when they see or engage in it. They are basically whatever you need to do in order to get your baby or toddler to sleep. For example, if you rock your baby all the way to sleep, "rocking" might be a sleep- association for your babe. If your child falls asleep drinking a bottle, then "drinking" or "sucking" might be a sleep-association for your kid. The key with sleep-associations is that you want them to be something that makes your child sleepy, but is also something that he or she can do on his own.

A bedtime routine is a type of sleep-association in that it is a series of events that trigger sleepiness in your child. That is why it works. The sleep-associations I am referencing here are the single things (like sucking on a pacifier, drinking a bottle, being held, or being rocked) that your child actually dozes off to. For example, I used to have to rock and bounce Rachel in order for her to fall asleep. She would actually close her eyes and fall asleep to the bouncy motion, just like a lot of other babies do. The problem was that, as she got older, she became too heavy to bounce for 30+ minutes. Furthermore, it was not something she could do for herself. When she woke up in the middle of the night, she needed me to bounce her again in order to fall asleep. This was a "bad" sleep-association.

The key is to let your baby fall asleep on his or her own, without you doing anything to help him or her. Whatever he does to fall asleep on his own becomes a "good" sleep-association because when he wakes up in the middle of the night, he will not need you to replicate anything… he can do it all by himself! This is essentially why cry-it-out and many sleep training methods are so effective, because they eliminate *you* as a sleep-association. When I tried weaning Rachel from bouncing and being held, she would cling to anything that had to do with me to fall asleep. As I worked with her, I quickly realized that neither the pacifier nor the bouncing were the problem, it was me holding or touching her! The comfort of my presence in the same room was not enough for her; she needed to grab on to something of mine.

So, if you want a Tot that sleeps through the night, the key starts with having him fall asleep on his own without your help. You need to break all of the "bad" sleep-associations and help him develop new ones that are pleasant, comforting, and do not require you in any way. If you can accomplish this at bedtime, then you will have less night-wakings as well and better sleep overall.

Working with Naps

Naps are a different kind of animal all together and totally separate from nighttime sleep. One of the things my sleep consultant shared with me is that daytime sleep and nighttime sleep are controlled by two different parts of the brain, and as such, you can have two different routines for the night and the day. Now, I do not know how true this is since I have never personally read research to support this, but I did obtain this information from experts in the field of child sleep, so I am sharing it with you here.

One of the things I hated most about naps as a working mom is that I had no control over them. I could not guarantee that my child's caregiver or daycare would ensure a nap, or put her down at the hour I requested, or make sure she napped sufficiently. I had to just go along with whatever form of a nap she got. I know I have mentioned this prior, so I won't go into it too much, but these are the realities of being a working parent. The suckiest part of all is that poor sleep during the day really does affect your child's sleep at night! So, if your caregiver is not putting your baby down for a nap as you have requested, then you get to pay the price with a child that will not fall asleep at night or wakes up all night long. If this is your situation, there is really little you can do about it... hate to tell you that. My suggestion is to focus your energy on having good weekend naps instead.

As I have mentioned previously, kids are quite intelligent, and they quickly figure out that there are different rules in different environments. This is why you may have a well-behaved child at school who is a terror at home. You can use this fact to your advantage with naps. Just because they are a "bad" napper at daycare does not mean they have to be a bad napper at home. Your child will learn that on the weekends at momma's or daddy's house, naps are done at a certain hour and in a certain way. It takes a little while for them to put the picture together clearly in their head because they are getting one routine at daycare and another at home. If you remain consistent, however, I promise your kiddo will eventually put it all together and get with the program.

Here are the tips I collected from other Mom's and Dad's to work on naps:

Tip #1: Have a Nap Time Routine

This is pretty much the same as the tip for bedtime. Try to put your child down for a nap roughly around the same hour every day by starting the routine around the same time and ending it around the same time. You also want to keep it simple and short like bedtime, and only include activities your baby enjoys. I would make sure your routine includes activities you don't mind doing several times in one day if your kid is taking more than one nap. For example, having a bath probably wouldn't be a good idea if your kid is still on 2-3 naps a day. A lullaby or a story, though, is a good choice because you can repeat that as many times as needed for those 2-3 naps.

Tip #2: Avoid Those Sleep-Associations!

Rachel was a terrible napper, just like she was a terrible bedtime sleeper. I remember the only way I could get her to sleep was by holding her in my arms. As a baby, I had her wrapped up in a Moby Wrap, which was totally necessary if I was going to get any studying done for school, and she used to nap in there like a dream. My mistake was not pulling her out once she was asleep, or trying to have her fall asleep out of the wrap. So what happened? She developed a sleep-association that required me to hold her the entire length of her nap! As a stay-at-home-mom, this may or may not have been an issue. But as a working mom, this was a BIG problem because I really needed to maximize my weekends to keep my house decently clean, and if I was holding a baby for two hours or more during naps, then I was not getting anything done.

When your child is a newborn, it is my opinion that it is completely fine to coddle them. This helps develop great attachment and is wonderful for bonding and developing trust. There comes a point, however, where you need to show your baby how to sleep on his own. And the older he gets, the harder it is to do. My suggestion is to try putting your child down while they are asleep. If they wake up, like Rachel did, then pick them up, soothe them, and try again. Eventually sleep will overwhelm them, and they will not wake up. As a working parent, this can be really tough because you have little time to accomplish everything you have to do on the weekends, and this process can be quite lengthy.

One idea to help you manage this is to work on those naps toward the very end of your maternity leave when you are home. You take several days to help your child practice naps, and hopefully, he will have mastered them before you go back to work. If, however, it does not happen, it is ok. You and your child will be just fine! I am not saying that it will be easy, but do not give up and do not despair.

Tip #3: Replicate the Night

This tip is easy and can make a really big difference for a lot of toddlers… make it dark! If you do not have black- out shutters or drapes, now is the time to invest in some. I remember I did not have a whole lot of money when Rachel was little, so I used beach towels to cover up her window. (Newspaper is also very effective, but can be time consuming.) You want to make the room where they nap nice and dark. The darkness sends signals to their brain that it is nighttime and that they should start to get sleepy. Combine this with your naptime routine and you should, hopefully, get some droopy eyes and little yawns signaling that it is time to sleep.

Thoughts on Co-Sleeping

Co-sleeping is a fairly controversial topic. Some people are adamantly against it, believing that co-sleeping with your child is engaging in child endangerment and should be avoided no matter what. (I even knew someone who wanted to call Child Protective Services on a family who was co-sleeping! Yikes!) Then, you have the other camp of people who believe co-sleeping is the only way to put your child to bed, and that failing to use this method is a cold and unloving way to parent your child.

The reality is that co-sleeping is not necessarily the best nor the worst method of putting your child to sleep. Research has shown that co-sleeping has many risks and benefits. Some of the risks revolve around the common fears that parents have of rolling over on top of the baby in the middle of the night and suffocating him, or of Sudden Infant Death Syndrome (SIDS). With regard to these fears, yes, it is true that you could roll over in the middle of the night, so always have caution. There are some new products now that you can buy in most retail stores that allow the baby to sleep in a small bed that you can place in between you and your partner. The bed separates you from the baby so that there is no fear of crushing the baby in the middle of the night, but you also get to keep your baby close all night long. As far as SIDS, however, the reality is that no one really knows what causes SIDS. As such, caution has been given to several potential culprits of SIDS, including bumpers in the crib, blankets or toys in the crib, sleeping on their tummies, co-sleeping, etc.

As mentioned, there are also many benefits to co-sleeping. Research has found that children who co-slept with their parents are more likely to have a higher self-esteem, are better behaved in school, have less anxiety,[2]

and have better attachment to their parental figures. For breastfeeding mothers, co-sleeping makes it easier to feed the baby in the night, making it less disruptive and more restful for mom and dad. Some research indicates that co-sleeping can even reduce the chances of SIDS fourfold![3]

As time continues, there is more and more research on co-sleeping. In the USA, the preferred method recommended by the American Academy of Pediatrics (AAP) remains that children and parents do not co-sleep. In 2016, however, the AAP changed their recommendations on Infant sleep for the first time since 2011! New research shows that infants should sleep in their parents' bedroom until 6 months of age, and

---

[2] P. Heron, "Non-Reactive Cosleeping and Child Behavior: Getting a Good Night's Sleep All Night, Every Night," Master's thesis, Department of Psychology, University of Bristol, 1994.

[3] P. S. Blair, P. J. Fleming, D. Bensley, et al., "Where Should Babies Sleep – Along or With Parents? Factors Influencing the Risk Of SIDS in the CESDI Study," British Medical Journal 319 (1999): 1457-1462.

preferably until 1 year of age. It is important to note, however, that the AAP still suggests that the infant should sleep in their own sleep-space, such as a crib or bassinet, in the parent's room.

As for me, I originally tried to avoid co-sleeping at all costs. My husband was terrified of co-sleeping for fear of rolling on the baby. I, myself, was not necessarily opposed to it because my own parents co-slept with me and my sisters. For my family and me, it was just a normal thing every parent does.

The bottom-line is, you have to do what is best for you and your family. Some parents enjoy the privacy of their bedroom and would rather not share that space with their children. This is fine! There is nothing wrong with this choice. I don't blame you for wanting to keep your own bed as YOUR bed. And for those who decide co-sleeping is the way to go for them, good for you! There is nothing wrong with that choice either! Both alternatives are viable options… and it's a personal choice. Don't feel bad about it, and don't feel the need to explain it to anyone.

Final Thoughts on Your Baby's Sleep

It is really hard when your child is not sleeping well, and you feel all of those chores and demands on your time just piling up around you. The worst is all those baby books that tell you to do it this way or that way, and make you feel awful if your kid isn't following "the plan." I always hated when those books would say, *"In about 3 days you'll notice an improvement in your child's sleep."* What they forget to mention is that the "improvement" might be as insignificant as your child crying for one minute less or sleeping for one minute more in his crib. Talk about frustrating! I remember thinking, *How can I call that an improvement! Nothing has changed!*

Managing sleep is probably one of the tasks that most parents hate and dread the most about having a baby. Don't get me wrong, some people have kids who just never have a problem with sleep. They are naturally "good" sleepers. I was not one of those parents, and I struggled with Rachel's sleep day after day.

The most important thing to remember is to never give up and don't lose hope. Your baby will sleep eventually, and you aren't doing anything wrong. Find whatever method works best for you, and stick with it. If it's co-sleeping, then co-sleep and don't look back. If it's cry-it-out, then go for it. The important thing is that you and your child get some restorative sleep that allows you both to function the following morning.

Don't compare your child to someone else's, and just smile and nod when others say, *"Well Bobby slept through the night when he was three months old."* Your child is unique, and your child will sleep when he or she is ready.

10. QUICK TIPS ON DISCIPLINE

One of the things I do most as a therapist is help parents manage their child's poor behavior. And I must say that I have seen some pretty bad stuff. I was thankful that Rachel wasn't too much of a handful, though she was willful and stubborn at times. The principles I taught my clients were the same things I used on my own daughter, and it's the same stuff that has been studied and proven by research.

Parenting is a tough job, and it's made harder when you work all day, come home, and then have to work with your toddler's tantrums. A lot of the kids I work with had nothing wrong with them… they just have parents who were so tired from working all day long that they don't discipline their kids consistently at night. I totally get this, being in the trenches myself. I don't want to go into the mechanics of discipline because I feel there are A LOT of books out there that will teach this to you. What I do want to do is give you some of the basics of the most popular tools, and some helpful "Therapist Insider" information that some parenting books just don't provide.

The Terrible Two's

In order to really get a handle on effective toddler discipline, it is important to understand what causes tantrums. The Terrible Two's can start as early as 18 months and last until about 3 ½ years of age. By the age of 4, most children have outgrown this stage, and they go back to the desire of pleasing their parents. During this time in a child's development, children are discovering themselves. They come to recognize that they have "needs" and "wants," and they also discover that there are certain activities they just don't like. Furthermore, they realize that they exist as an independent person, separate from you or anyone else. As such, they become **egocentric**, meaning that it is all about them, all the time! Hence, you will start hearing things like, *"That's mine,"* or *"I want that,"* or *"Give it to me!"* Sound familiar? The words "I," "Me," or "Mine" will become very popular, and used in almost any phrase or sentence they say.

Now, the Terrible Two's are considered "terrible," because children begin having tantrums at this stage. You might witness crying, kicking, screaming, hitting, biting, or watch the child throw himself on the floor. These behaviors are normal and to be expected. There are many reasons why toddlers will engage in these behaviors, so let's review those:

1.   **Inability to Communicate:** Most toddlers around this age lack the ability to effectively communicate

their wants and needs. They lack an expansive vocabulary and struggle to communicate their feelings to others. As a result, children become frustrated, which then turns into negative behaviors that develop into tantrums.

2.   **Poor Modeling**:   Another potential reason for tantruming is poor modeling from parents or other important, adult role-models. Most adults will raise their voice when they are angry or may "storm off" when they are upset. Some adults will slam doors, throw papers on the floor, or simply toss objects that they are holding in an aggressive manner. When you think about it, that is simply an adult tantrum.   If your children are watching you engage in that behavior, they will assume that the appropriate way to communicate their own anger or frustrations to others is by imitating these same behaviors. If you are unsure whether you are guilty of this (HINT: *Most adults are!*), ask someone who knows you personally and has frequently seen you during times of anger or frustration.   Let an objective person share with you what they have seen. Don't be upset if it is not the answer you were hoping for!

3.   **Impulsivity & Poor Emotion Regulation:** Children at this age have a very difficult time controlling their emotions and behaviors. A large part of this has to do with impulsivity. Most toddlers are very impulsive and will simply act out thoughts or ideas that come to their mind without stopping to think about the consequences of their behavior(s). The reason why young children are so impulsive is because the part of the brain that helps a person

assess consequences is not completely developed yet. In fact, researchers believe that this part of the brain is not fully developed until sometime in the early 20's, which is why teenagers also engage in impulsive acts too. This part of the brain does develop over time, however, so a child's ability to assess the outcome of any given event will improve over the course of time as they grow older.

Emotion Regulation is the ability to control and moderate one's emotions. Think of the knobs on your stove that control the temperature of the burners. You can turn the knob to increase the heat or lower the heat until you get the temperature you need. Very expensive stoves have temperature regulators that are very accurate, but cheaper models struggle more. Small children are like a cheaper stove in that they go from cool, calm, and collect, to very hot, angry, and out of control with even the smallest of adjustments. As such, simple things will set toddlers off into a tizzy.

4. **Parental Reaction:** Finally, once a child has begun to raise his voice or act out, parents tend to respond with anger and frustration. Adults will yell back, spank or hit, or they might even threaten their children (i.e. *If you don't do ABC, I'm going to XYZ to you*). Unfortunately, most of these reactions only cause toddlers to become more upset, and pushes them into a tantrum or worsens the tantrum. Furthermore, these reactions model these negative behaviors back to the child (see point 2 above) and creates a vicious cycle that rarely gets better.

5. **Inconsistent Discipline:** Probably one of the biggest problems that parents face is the inability to remain consistent. In my work as a therapist, inconsistent parenting/discipline is probably the number one problem parents have when it comes to children who are defiant, disruptive, rude, etc. Many parents are busy, nowadays, working two jobs and managing a multitude of different responsibilities. This results in parents who are tired and lack enough drive and motivation to keep up and maintain their own rules and limits. I truly feel for these parents!

There are more reasons that children tantrum, but these are basic ones I encountered when working with families. Understanding why children have tantrums is important to helping you keep calm as a parent when these situations arise in your own home.

So, now that you have a brief idea of the causes of these behaviors, let's talk about tips that can help you manage them in your own life.

Tip # 1: All Children are Different

All children are different. This seems pretty basic, right? I mean, I think we all understand that every child is unique, and yet, most parents have a hard time really grasping the root of this statement. I can't tell you how many times I have parents say to me, *"Bobby is out of control! His brother is just perfect! I don't get what the problem is... I treat them the same, so it must be an issue with Bobby."* Sorry, but this is flawed thinking. If you really understood the concept that *all children are different,* then you would also understand that nothing is <u>wrong</u> with Bobby. Bobby just requires a different parenting style or technique. The hard part is finding the technique that works best for Bobby.

In a situation like the one above with Bobby, I would say that, about 95% of the time, the parents are NOT treating the kids the same even if they think they are. Remember that, as time goes on, your skills as a parent, the amount of time you have available, and your financial situation are all different. You might not even be living in the same home when your first child was born or have the same job, etc. As such, you change as a parent. Things that used to be important, no longer are, and things you did not care about might suddenly have new meaning. Thus, when you are parenting multiple kids, different results are produced in the behavior of those children. If this is your situation, try enlisting friends who you trust to observe you and let you know if you are really treating both kids equally. Don't become offended or get upset if the answer is not what you want to hear. Instead, take the information and see how you can adjust your parenting or interactions with your children so that you get the result you want.

Tip # 2: Trial-Runs Should Go for at Least One Month

When I teach parents a new parenting style or technique, most of them give it a go for about 1-2 weeks before coming to me and saying, "It didn't work!" The reality is that kids take several weeks to adjust to new rules or styles, and they will test you consistently to see if the rules have changed. Whenever you adopt a new disciplining method, you have to give it at least one to two months before you throw in the towel.

As a therapist, I find that, on average, it takes two months of trying a new disciplining technique *consistently* before the children have completely adjusted. By the one month mark, however, you should be able to see some significant differences going in the direction that you are hoping for. If you do not, review what you have been doing. Once again, rely on friends or family who are more likely to have an objective opinion to report back to you on your progress. Have you been sticking to the new plan *consistently*? If so, then you might try it a little longer or try something new altogether if you're not seeing any results.

Tip #3: Do Not Fall Prey to Relapses

A **relapse** is when you see the undesirable behavior disappear for a while and then, all of a sudden, it comes back with a vengeance! You will know you had a relapse because you will have the *"we take one step forward and two steps back"* thought go through your head. Relapses are common in the mental health field, but they are also super common when it comes to behavioral changes in kids. When you hit a relapse, you can't give up! If you quit, thinking *"It didn't work,"* you will actually be doing yourself a disservice. Here is why:

Every time you throw in the towel when you hit a relapse, you will teach your child that you, the parent, have a breaking point. And if <u>he</u>, the child, can get you to your breaking point, then <u>you</u> give up and <u>he</u> does not have to follow the rules anymore.

It is that simple folks, and it is probably the single biggest problem most parents have when it comes to disciplining children, especially willful ones.

Whenever you hit a relapse, you need to become MORE STUBBORN than your toddler. Stick to the rules more firmly and discipline more consistently. Relapses are tests, and your kid might choose to test you every day for several weeks to see if they can push you to your breaking point. If you stick with it, and remind yourself that this is nothing more than a power-play coming from your child, then you will overcome it! Relapses will become less frequent and will be less severe each time until they do not come along anymore and become extinct.

Tip #4: Explain to Your Child What They Did Wrong

When you discipline your child, please explain to them what they did wrong. It is very easy to say, *"You hit your brother! You get a time-out!"* Kids really need to be taught *why* the behavior is bad, and what the behavior is you would like to see in the future.

Here is an example:

If you have a child who hits when she does not get her way, sit her down and say something to the effect of, *"Sally, hitting hurts other people. Do you like it when Ruby hits you? No, right? Well, other people do not like it when you hit them either. I know you were angry, and that is ok. Mommy gets angry too sometimes, and you are allowed to get angry. But when you are angry, you cannot hit. Next time, when you get angry, walk away and take 10 deep breaths. If you still feel angry, find me and I will help you."*

Make sure you make the conversation age appropriate and the interventions (like deep breathing) age appropriate too. Finally, do not have this conversation while your child is in the middle of a tantrum. It will not help the situation! Wait until your child has calmed down before you talk with them.

Tip #5: Do Not Squelch Your Child's Emotions

Something I find very common in therapy is that parents do not like their kids getting angry about stuff. They complain to me because, *"Sally screams when 'X' happens."* Of course she screams... she is angry. I always remind parents that when they discipline, they need to help their children develop a language for their emotions and then let their child know that it is alright to experience those emotions. In the example in Tip #4, notice that the parent name's the emotion (i.e. anger), and acknowledges that this emotion is *ok* to feel. The key to discipline is to NOT squelch out certain emotions, but to help teach your child *how* to properly EXPRESS the emotion they feel. We do this in 3 ways:

1. Highlighting the emotion

2. Validating the emotion

3. Teaching appropriate self-expression for the emotion

Many times, I would tell Rachel, *"I know you are upset, and it is ok to be mad at Mommy. But screaming is not an ok way of showing this feeling. You are allowed to cry, and you are allowed to tell Mommy you are mad, but screaming is not ok."* I began talking to my daughter like this since she was about a year old. I can't even begin to tell you how much I was criticized for this by family and strangers. I remember one day, I was speaking to my daughter about her behavior, only to have an elderly woman come to me and say, *"Honey, she doesn't know what you're saying. She's only a baby."* I responded to her concern by stating, *"I know, but if I practice good disciplining techniques now, it will become second nature to me. Then, when she's older, I will already be in good practice with the parenting skills I want to use."* The look on this woman's face was absolutely priceless. I am pretty sure she thought I was nuts, but little did she know that I was a therapist who specialized in parenting.

What most of your family and friends do not realize is that our children understand language much sooner than they can speak it. And, even if you do not think your child understands, explaining to your child what they did wrong and what the correct behavior is from the beginning helps to set the stage for future discipline. It also helps to get you in the habit of doing it. Trust me, it will save you from a lot of grief later!

Tip #6: Do Not Forget the Value of Time-Outs

A **time-out** is one of the most well-known and effective disciplining methods out there, but unfortunately, most parents do them wrong. There are a few different variations to time-outs, but the one I am going to teach you is one of the most common and one of the most effective. Time-outs can be used with a child as early as 1 ½ years old, and remains effective through most of the elementary school years. Some children in middle school can still benefit from a time-out, but most kids outgrow this method around that time. The hope is that, if you manage your child's behaviors early on (i.e. toddler years), then those middle-school days will not present too much of a problem.

Let us begin by discussing the appropriate length of time for a time-out. This is actually fairly easy to remember: A time-out is 1 minute for every year of life. This means that if you have a 2 year old, he gets a 2-minute time-out. If your child is 8 years old, then she gets an 8-minute time-out. Nothing longer, nothing shorter, and no ½ minutes either (i.e. a 1 ½ year old still gets a 1-minute time-out). Finally, time-outs should not exceed 10 minutes. So if your child is 11 years old, do not give them an 11-minute time-out. Research has shown that time-outs longer than 10 minutes do not produce a better effect on children, and some research even shows that it could be detrimental.

Once you figure out how long your child's time-out should be, take a timer (you can find them pretty cheap), set it to the appropriate length of time, and tell your child that he can't get up from the "Time-Out Spot" until the timer goes off. He is allowed to console himself, but is not allowed to engage in aggressive physical or verbal behaviors during time-outs. If he speaks aggressively (i.e. *"I hate you,"* etc.) or becomes physically aggressive (i.e. throws objects from the Time-Out Spot, etc.), the time starts over. If he gets up from his spot to go grab something, the time starts over again. During a time-out, your tot should sit and remain respectful towards you and others.

Finally, the time does not begin until your child has sat down politely in the spot you designated. So, if you say "time-out" and they start tantruming, you wait until the tantrum is over. Once it is over, then the time begins. Remember that, for very young children, you might want to be a little more lax on this rule.

Time-outs can be hard to do because many kids will test their parents over and over again to see if mommy or daddy are really serious. Most of my clients said their kid tested them about 3-4 different times before finally giving in and accepting their time-out politely. I should also say that, just because your child has a fit when you delve out a time-out, it does not mean you "add time" to the time-out. He still only gets 1 minute per year of life.

Once the time-out has been served, be sure to talk to your child about what he did wrong and what behavior you would like to see next time. Make sure you are realistic and age appropriate in your discussion. After this, make sure to give your child a hug, kiss, reassurance, and then send him on his way. Time has been served and the wrong-doing should be forgiven and never mentioned again.

Now, time-outs can be tough to serve if you are in a restaurant or a store. Most professionals recommend time-outs being served immediately after the act, but that may not always be possible. You can go two ways with this particular issue:

1. You can either serve the time-out wherever you are at.

2. You can serve it later once you get home.

The first option is the best, but it can be difficult. I had a girlfriend who would have her son serve the time-out wherever he was at. She was in a supermarket once and he had to sit in Aisle 3 for his 10 minutes. She just shopped around him. A co-worker of mine would drop everything he was doing, grab his child, and take her outside to the car where she had to serve her time-out. Once the time-out was over, they would go back into the store or restaurant and go on with their day.

The first method is certainly effective, but I find that working parents struggle with it. So, I began using the second method with my clients and found that, if it was done right, it worked just as well. If you are at the market, and your child acts up, you point out to them that they are getting a time-out when you get home due to their behavior. When you get home, you remind the child of the behavior that led to a time-out and then follow through with it. This specific method is not as effective with very small children, but I find that school-aged kids benefit from this method just as well. Again, this is not the *best* method, but it will work in a pinch.

Finally, you can serve time-outs with objects too, not just with your kids. I find this incredibly helpful when we are out shopping or eating out. For example, one evening, when Rachel was about 2 years old, we were eating at a local restaurant when Rachel started acting up. She was throwing her crayons and coloring the table instead of her paper. I warned her to stop coloring the table. She kept coloring anyways. So I asked her to look at me, and then warned her a second time, but this time stating, *"If you color the table again, I will take the crayons away."* She obeyed and colored on her paper for a moment before going right back to coloring the table. I then proceed to take the crayons and told her, *"Because you are coloring the table and not listening to Mommy, I am taking the crayons away for 2 minutes."* She cried, but I kept those crayons for a full two minutes. Once the time was up, I waited until she calmed down before returning the crayons. Once she was calm, I reminded her not to color the table again, and I warned her that if she began to color the table once more, I would take the crayons away for another 2 minutes.

In this above example, I did not give Rachel a time-out, rather I gave the *crayons* a time-out. I took them away from her for two minutes. If she was 3 years old, I would have taken the crayons away for 3 minutes, just like a regular time-out. This is helpful when out and about, and can also be very effective if you use it right. I use both methods for Rachel. If I am home, I typically use "body" time-outs if she is misbehaving, and "object" time-outs for minor issues, if applicable. This combination gave me some more options for discipline, and helped give me more flexibility when out running errands.

Finally, the most common problem parents encounter when first attempting time-outs is that the child will not stay in the Time-Out Spot. If this is your situation, simply pick the child up and move them back to the time-out location. You should do this every time the child leaves the spot. At this point, you also restart the time on the clock as well. For example, I was babysitting my nephew (6 years old at the time), and after he misbehaved, I gave him a time-out. He was not familiar with this technique, so of course, he left the Time-Out Spot while throwing a tantrum. I calmly informed him that he was to remain in the Time-Out Spot (i.e. my laundry room) until his time had been served. When he refused to return to the Time-Out Spot, I simply picked him up and put him in the spot again. He ran from the spot a second time, throwing another tantrum. I repeated my explanation of time-outs, and carried him again to the Time-Out Spot. He ran from the Time-Out Spot 4 times that day, and every time I returned him to the same spot and explained the time-out procedure. I also restarted the timer every time, explaining to him why I was restarting the time. Eventually, he remained in the Time-Out Spot and served his time gracefully. Naturally, he was not very happy with me, but ever since that day, he is much more cautious about misbehaving when I am babysitting him.

Tip #7: Be Cautious of "Warnings" & Do Not Forget to Follow Through!

The last part we should talk about with regard to time-outs (or any disciplining method you choose) is warnings. Every parent gives out warnings, and truly, they are not a bad idea. They give your child the opportunity to check their behavior and correct it without being disciplined. But they can also be a child's ticket out of trouble, which just means more trouble for you!

As a therapist, I usually recommend one warning. If the behavior does not change after your warning, then you need to follow through with your discipline tactic. I highly discourage multiple warnings because if kids get used to it, then THEY WILL NOT LISTEN TO YOU the first time you tell them to stop. This only increases your frustration, and makes you less able to effectively delve out discipline when you need to. Take this following example:

"Johnny, stop jumping on the sofa. I'm warning you, if you jump on it again, I will take away your toy. Johnny! I told you to stop! Do you really want your toy taken away? That's it! I'm going to take it away!" Then Johnny screams and begs his mom not to. He promises to be good and to stop jumping on the sofa. His mom lets him go and then about 5-10 minutes later, he's jumping on the sofa again.

There are way too many warnings being offered to this child, and because there are so many warnings, he does not listen the first, second, or even third time the warnings are given. This happens because he believes mommy will give a fourth, fifth, and sixth warning before actually taking his toy away. He begins to question whether or not she really meant it when she said "stop." The best way to avoid this situation is to simply give one warning, and then delve whatever discipline is necessary if your child does the behavior again.

Along these similar lines, let us talk about follow through. I had a girlfriend once who threatened her toddler with giving away his food to another kid if he did not finish eating. It worked great because he would gobble everything up. The error in this threat, however, is that she had no intention of following through with it if he did not listen to her warning.

Whenever you threaten your child with a time-out, a toy being taken away, getting up and leaving the party early, pulling the car over, etc., you MUST go through with it! If you do not, your child will begin questioning whether or not you really mean what you say. They second guess you and your warnings or threats. This only makes you less effective as a parent later. As your child gets older, they will begin to understand that there are certain actions you will not follow through on, so they stop listening. Do not fall prey to this!

Always remember to give threats or warnings you can actually follow through on. For example, if you know you are not going to leave the party early, then threaten a time-out in the car or no birthday cake instead. If you are at a restaurant, do not threaten, *"You can't have dinner,"* because you *know* you are not going to let your child go hungry. Instead, threaten no dessert or no french fries. These threats and warnings make just as big of an impression on your child and are more effective because you can actually manage them as a parent. So, think a little smaller and remember to always follow through!

Tip #8: Do Not Forget to Reward Good Behavior

It is really easy to yell and scold children when they do something wrong. It is a lot harder to remember to reward them when they do something right! Research has shown that focusing on and rewarding good behavior is more effective than punishing bad behavior. If this is the case, however, why don't people do this more often? The simple answer is that it is actually really difficult to remember to reward our children when they are doing exactly as they are told. If you are running around trying to get dinner on the table after work, you rarely notice little Cindy coloring peacefully in her coloring book. You glance at her, notice she is coloring, and move on with dinner. But, if Cindy starts to paint the walls red, you will stop everything you are doing to stop her in her tracks! We give the attention to the bad behavior, and we fail to give positive attention when she is behaving well.

I think all parents are guilty of this at one point or another, and that includes me! There have been many times when Rachel was being a good girl, playing quietly or expressing her anger in appropriate ways, and I forgot to say, *"Thank you for being a good girl and playing nicely."*

This tip is an important one if you can remember to do it, because by rewarding good behavior (or at least acknowledging your child and letting them know you appreciate their good behavior in that moment), you actually encourage your children to display more of that same good behavior! Kids would much rather get prizes and rewards over punishments and time-outs… trust me!

Tip #9: Model the Behavior You Want to See

This is my last tip to you, and it is a big one: be a good role model! I mentioned this earlier in this section, but I want to talk a little more about it because it is truly an important part of parenting and discipline. We all know that children are tiny copycats, mimicking everything we do. This goes for the good stuff we do, like saying our "please" and "thank you's," and the bad stuff too! Many of the parents I work with have a habit of yelling at their kids when they are angry with them. This is actually unnecessary and only teaches them to yell back in return. Usually, a firm tone of voice and a face displaying displeasure is enough to get the idea across. Yelling does not really add anything to the mix, except for fear. Now, just because you yell at your kids every once in a while does not mean you have ruined them for life. A lot of disciplining with frequent shouting and yelling, however, really sets a bad example and creates a home environment that provokes a lot of anxiety.

If your child has a habit of yelling at you during tantrums, take a step back and look at yourself. Do you and your spouse yell at each other during fights and arguments? Do you or your partner yell at your child when he does something wrong? If you answered "yes" to any of these, then you have an idea of where your tot is getting the message that yelling is the appropriate way to display anger or displeasure. The same idea goes for walking away from you while you are talking, slamming doors, stomping upstairs, hitting, throwing, etc. Yes, movies and video games can also teach them some bad habits, but the reality is that, it starts with you!

So, double check yourself and make sure you keep your cool when you discipline your child or argue with your partner. Always remember, you have a little pair of eyes watching you, taking you as his or her prime example of how to manage their own emotions and problematic situations.

I hope this chapter has been helpful. If you haven't done so already, you can get my book, *Eliminating Temper Tantrums: 4 Keys to Mastering Your Child's Anger Outbursts*, where I go into great depth on effective discipline strategies. I also explain my approach to using discipline as a tool to create a harmonious household and a loving Parent-Child Relationship. You can download this book for free at:

www.kcdreisbach.com/gift-free-ebook

11. THE SILENT PREDATORS: DEPRESSION, ANXIETY, & PSYCHOSIS

When you are pregnant for the first time, you are promised by others that you will experience these blissful moments with your soon-to-arrive new baby, filled with love, joy, and sweet peace. Yes, you will be tired and stressed, as all new parents are, but at the end of the day, love, joy, and peace would be yours. One of the most disturbing things for me to experience once my baby was born was the utter stress, depression, and anxiety I felt instead of this love, joy, and peace.

Rachel was not an easy baby. She was not a "colicky" baby, but she was not easy either. Although I knew I loved her, I also felt this odd detachment from her. I wanted her to be safe and I stressed over everything that had to do with her, but at the same time, I felt this numbness. I remember being so tired. I remember feeling so stressed and anxious, and I remember crying in the shower as feelings of sadness, guilt, and shame filled my heart. I remember feeling alone.

Having all of these thoughts, feelings, and emotions, I remember thinking to myself, *Why didn't anyone tell me? Why did everyone lie to me and promise me such sweet joy when the reality was only pain?* And I would think to myself, *Maybe something is wrong with me. Maybe I am a bad mother! Maybe I was never cut out to do this!* And then the guilt would hit, along with feelings of shamefulness. My older sister wanted a baby so badly, but due to infertility issues, she was not able to get pregnant. And here I was, her younger sister with this new baby that I was beginning to resent! What kind of a mother was I?!?

Later, as the stresses of being a new parent wore off, and as I began to figure out who I was as a mother, I began to find myself once again. I found myself connected with my baby, and I finally began experiencing those blissful moments with Rachel of love, joy, and sweet peace. But it was a rough road in getting there… and it was a lonely one. Did I suffer from Post-Partum Depression? No, I don't think so, but… maybe. Was it the infamous Baby Blues? Yes, but it was more than that too. Was I crazy? Nope… just human.

Eventually, I graduated from my Master's degree in Marital and Family Therapy and found my first job as a therapist. There, I received trainings on all kinds of topics, but one of the most enlightening was a training I received on maternal mental health. I found that I could identify with many of the symptoms listed for several of the maternal mental health disorders, and I finally figured out that, with a little extra emotional help and support, raising Rachel for those first 12 months could have been so much easier. But therein lies the problem... no one talks about these issues. It took a specialized degree in mental health *and* additional, professional training for me to finally understand my own experiences as a new mom. After that training, I began seeking out more, wanting to learn about these issues in the hopes that I could help other new parents understand their own experiences.

A New Baby: The Bittersweet Experience

You might be surprised by how many women and men suffer from depression, horrific intrusive thoughts, and anxiety when their new baby enters their world. Although they love their child, they are also in deep emotional pain and distress caused by genetic and environmental factors, as well as hormones. Many of these souls deal with these emotions in secret, afraid of what others might think of them if they shared their experience. The unfortunate thing is that suffering through this alone only makes it worse. The guilt of not feeling "attached" to your baby, the shame of not wanting to hold, play, or engage with your baby can be debilitating. It is for this reason that I wanted to tackle this topic in this book.

While raising Rachel, I experienced some of these issues and symptoms, though not nearly enough to truly understand the anguish that some new parents go through. And if you are one of these parents, I want you to know that you are not alone! Please know that there is help and there is a way out of this misery! The mental health disorders that I will be sharing with you are very treatable and curable. There is nothing wrong or shameful in admitting that you need a little help.

The Baby Blues

Most women experience some form of the "baby blues" after their child arrives, and many men do too! Due to huge hormonal shifts caused by labor and delivery, many moms will experience frequent emotional highs and lows, going up and down between joy and sadness. It is important to note that this is completely normal, even for men, because we have now found that dads experience hormonal shifts after birth too!

Approximately 80% of new moms experience, what is frequently called, the "Baby Blues" during their first 2 weeks post-partum. (That's A LOT of women!) Dads can also get the Baby Blues too, with approximately 1 in 10 men experiencing these symptoms after their child is born. (Check out Postpartum Support International at www.postpartum.net for more info.)

Symptoms of the Baby Blues consist of mood swings, tearfulness, being hyper-vigilant (essentially "being on edge" or "jumpy"), or being reactive (think of this like being "snappy" or perhaps "temperamental"). These symptoms look a lot like PMS and will typically last about two to three weeks after the baby is born. Symptoms may also include irritability, crying spells, anxiety, inability to sleep, mood swings, and exhaustion. The Baby Blues is also very treatable and does not require anything other than rest, good nutrition (especially if you are nursing or pumping breast milk), exercise, and lots of support and TLC from friends and family.

After those first few weeks, the symptoms should subside and go away completely. If symptoms persist, however, or feel severe in nature, you may not be experiencing the Baby Blues, and might actually be suffering from a maternal (or paternal!) mental health disorder.

Maternal & Paternal Mental Health Disorders

It is important to note that any new parent is vulnerable to a maternal/paternal mental health disorder, including adoptive parents, foster parents, etc. The most at risk, however, are women who have delivered a baby because the huge hormonal shift that occurs after delivery complicates the situation a bit.

As mentioned, these disorders can happen to dads as well, but are much more likely to occur to mom. As such, and for the sake of ease, I will be discussing these disorders in terms of "maternal" mental health. Do remember, though, that all new parents are at risk, regardless of gender or who actually gave birth to the child (i.e. adopted, foster, etc.)

There are four maternal mental health disorders. Most people know of at least one of these disorders: Postpartum Depression. So, we will start there. Afterwards, I will discuss Postpartum Anxiety, Perinatal OCD, and Postpartum Psychosis. All four can be severe, moderate, or mild, but only Postpartum Psychosis is extremely dangerous and requires immediate (and quite possibly emergency) treatment regardless of the severity level. Also note that, although I list symptoms and warning signs, do not self-diagnose or diagnose your partner or loved-one. If, after reading some of these symptoms or warning signs, you feel that you or someone you know might suffer from one of these disorders, please seek help from a mental health professional immediately.

Postpartum Depression

Postpartum Depression (PPD) is one of the best known disorders, and it is often blamed as the culprit behind mothers who kill their infants or children. It is extremely common; so common in fact, that it is the number one complication of childbirth! *Number ONE!* Statistics show that approximately 1 million women per year will suffer from this condition, but most feel so ashamed or afraid to admit that they are suffering from depression after their baby is born, they don't get the help that they desperately need or deserve.

The following is a list of symptoms commonly associated with Postpartum Depression:

o   Tearfulness and Crying
o   Sad or Depressed Mood
o   Lack of Desire, Interest, or Motivation
o   Lack of Joy or Pleasure in Activities
o   Feelings of Extreme Stress or Feeling Overwhelmed
o   Exhaustion
o   Sleep Problems (*Note: Most new parents have sleep problems because their new baby does not sleep. What I am referring to here is when a parent does not sleep, even when they have the opportunity to do so.)
o   Changes in Appetite (*Note: Either they do not

eat at all or they eat all the time. We are looking for a <u>change</u> in their eating habits. It does not matter in which direction.)

o   Mood Swings
o   Anxiety
o   Anger or Irritability
o   Poor Concentration or Poor Focus
o   Isolating from Others
o   Feelings of Worthlessness, Hopelessness, or Helplessness
o   Feelings of Guilt or Shame (*Note: Usually the guilt and shame is surrounded around the fact that the parent can't feel connected to her baby, or she feels ashamed that she is not happy about having the baby.)
o   Suicidal Thoughts (Example: "I just wish I could close my eyes and never wake-up," or "I wish I were dead.")
o   Not Wanting to Hold the Baby
o   Lack of Feelings toward the Baby (Examples: feeling detached, numb, etc.)

It is important to note that these symptoms can pop up at any time during the first year of the baby's life! So, just because your baby is now 6 months old, it does not mean that you are "out of the woods" just yet. If, after reading this list, you find yourself nodding and saying, *"Yup, I do that,"* or *"Mmhmm, I feel like that,"* then please seek help! You do not have to do this alone, and you do not have to feel ashamed or guilty. You are *not* a bad parent for experiencing these symptoms. You are human! And you deserve to love your postpartum days, not suffer in quiet agony. Please, get help....

Postpartum Anxiety

Let's start talking about some lesser known maternal mental health disorders that are also pretty common. Postpartum Anxiety (PPA), also sometimes referred as "postpartum depression with anxiety," consists of many anxiety symptoms and may also include panic attack symptoms. PPA, although incredibly uncomfortable, does not typically produce the same level of shame or guilt that moms will experience with Postpartum Depression. But parents suffering from PPA might feel more embarrassed by their symptoms, and so they may never seek out help. As such, they tend to suffer in silence. You might notice that many of the symptoms of PPA overlap with the symptoms for Postpartum Depression, but they are, in fact, different diagnoses. This is why it is important to consult with a mental health professional that is trained to differentiate between these two disorders.

The following is a list of symptoms commonly associated with PPA:

o Feelings of Agitation or Irritability
o In Ability to Sit Still
o Hyper-vigilance or Feeling "On Edge"
o Excessive and Consistent Worry about the Baby or herself
o Sleep Problems (*Note: Again, we are looking for an inability to sleep, even when the parent has the opportunity to do so!)
o Changes in Appetite (*Note: Again, either the parent does not eat at all or she eats all the time. Remember, it is the change we are looking for.)
o Racing Thoughts

- o Accelerated Heart Rate or Heart Palpitations
- o Shortness of Breath or Difficulty Breathing Deeply

The following is a list of symptoms commonly associated with Panic Attacks:

- o Feeling Panicky or Extremely Anxious
- o Dizziness
- o Shortness of Breath or Difficulty Breathing
- o Sensations of Choking or Inability to Breath
- o Chest Pains, Racing Heart, or Heart Palpitations
- o Agitation or Irritability
- o Restlessness or Inability to Sit Still
- o Feelings of Going Numb or Tingling Sensations
- o Hot or Cold Flashes
- o Sweating

Moms suffering from Postpartum Anxiety will oftentimes be dismissed by their friends and family as simply being a "worry wart" or a "helicopter parent," which is incredibly frustrating for these mothers since their feelings are often invalidated and brushed aside. These parents frequently feel embarrassed about their worry and anxiety, and they may try to hide it in an attempt to "fit in" or be the parent that everyone else expects them to be. If you feel like this list describes you, please seek help. Anxiety is immensely uncomfortable, and there is no reason for you to have to endure it.

Perinatal OCD

Perinatal Obsessive Compulsive Disorder (Perinatal OCD), also sometimes known as "postpartum depression with obsessive compulsive features," is a very uncomfortable mental health disorder and usually occurs with depression too. There are many types of "OCD" disorders, including Obsessive Compulsive Disorder (OCD) and Obsessive Compulsive Personality Disorder (OCPD), which are both already recognized as distinct diagnoses by mental health professionals. Perinatal OCD has many of the same symptoms as OCD, but what makes them different has to do with the "onset" (i.e. when it first started) of the disorder, as well as the *type* of obsession or compulsion the person has. The worst part of this disorder, in my opinion, is the type of intrusive thoughts moms can get, and the guilt and shame that come along with those thoughts.

The following is a list of symptoms commonly associated with the "Obsessions" of Perinatal OCD:

- o **Contamination:** These are intrusive thoughts about germs, viruses, bacteria, etc. It frequently comes along with fear of bottles not being "clean" enough, or that the baby will get sick if someone looks at the baby the wrong way, etc. Basically, you are incredibly worried and "obsessed" about the baby, or baby-stuff, being "contaminated" with something bad.

- o **Doubting:** These are intrusive thoughts related to not having done something right or forgetting to do something important, etc. In this situation, you find yourself constantly checking and obsessing about everything because you "doubt" yourself or your partner. (For example: *"Did you check the temperature of the bottle? Are you sure!?"*)

o **Sexual & Harming:** These intrusive thoughts are incredibly disturbing for the mother, and will frequently lead to mom feeling depressed. These are typically vivid thoughts of mom hurting her baby or sexually molesting her child. Many moms who have this will have detailed mental pictures in their minds that scare them and bring about fear, shame, and guilt. It is incredibly important to note that moms that have these thoughts *have no intention or desire to do these things!!!* These moms are *horrified* and might avoid their child for fear of their own thoughts! It is a very distressing thing for parents, and these moms will frequently suffer alone for fear that they will be rejected or deemed as an unfit mother by friends or family.

The following is a list of symptoms commonly associated with the "Compulsions" of Perinatal OCD:

o Frequent Checking & Re-Checking
o Frequent Washing
o Avoidance
o Seeking Reassurance from Others (i.e. "Did this ever happen to you when you had your baby?")
o Any behavior Mom engages in to avoid harm or minimize triggers for her intrusive thoughts (i.e. obsessions)

I mentioned earlier that I had more than the Baby Blues, but not necessarily Postpartum Depression (in the classical sense) while raising Rachel. It is my belief that I, unfortunately, suffered from a mild case of Perinatal OCD. And my obsessive thoughts were all of the above! I worried that she was going to get sick, so I always felt my stomach do summersaults every time my little niece and nephew wanted to hold her. Sometimes the anxiety would be so bad that, as I watched them touch her face with their hands, I would often feel as though I was going to throw-up. I knew they were not doing anything wrong, and I knew my fears were a little irrational, but that knowledge did nothing to settle my stomach. The silly part is that I would never say anything and would simply grin-and-bear it because I was so embarrassed. I did not want my family to think I was nuts, or just some "over-protective" parent. So, I just dealt with it.

I also had doubting obsessions, usually that my husband was not doing something right or forgetting to do something important. I also had those doubting obsessions when people babysat Rachel. Having someone else, other than me, watch Rachel made my skin want to crawl! I was always terrified that something bad was going to happen to her under someone else's watch, and that my relationship with that person would forever be destroyed. The result was that I hardly ever asked for help. I would not ask my husband to watch her when she cried at three o'clock in the morning, I would not have Grandma babysit her on the weekends, and I would not ask someone to watch her so I could get a shower. The problem with this whole scenario was feeling stressed, overwhelmed, and so incredibly exhausted each and every day. Eventually, I physically just could not do it anymore, and I had to let someone else watch her, but not without constantly worrying about Rachel every second we were apart.

Lastly, I suffered from harming obsessions as well, and these, of course, were the worst. When Rachel would cry hour after hour without stopping in the middle of the night, I would have horrible thoughts of shaking her, throwing her against a wall, or smothering her with a pillow. I remember hating myself for having these thoughts. I knew I *did not* want to do these things. In fact, I remember sobbing as I held her those late nights, feeling like I was going crazy because I was having these horrific scenes playing out in my head. Usually, it was when I was having these thoughts that I would desperately wake my husband and ask him to watch her. Although I never told him about the intrusive thoughts I was having for fear of what he would think of me, I would tell him I could not do it anymore and beg him to take her. Most nights he would, but sometimes he just couldn't do it either. So again, I endured.

To put your mind at ease, I never hurt Rachel. In fact, I never even spanked her as a form of discipline. I never harmed her, despite these horrid images and thoughts because I loved my daughter so much, and I never wanted to harm her. Remember earlier when I described "sexual & harming" obsessive thoughts? The important thing I pointed out was that moms who suffer from this, DO NOT WANT TO HARM THEIR CHILDREN. And this is why they feel such shame and guilt, which is what I felt too.

I never told anyone about these thoughts I had, especially the harming ones, because I felt like no one would understand. I felt like I would be judged, hated, ridiculed, made-fun-of, lectured, or my greatest fear, that someone would take my daughter away from me. It was not until I became a mental health professional and received extensive training on maternal mental health issues that I finally understood what I experienced.

From one mom to another, if you are suffering through this, you do not have to do it alone! Research has found that 9% of new mothers will meet criteria for a diagnosis of OCD[4] (specifically Perinatal OCD), and many of these women never get help (myself included). I am here to tell you that you do not have to do it alone. Perinatal OCD is treatable, and it can go away if you get the right support and treatment. Please... seek help!

Perinatal Psychosis

Of all of these mental health disorders, Perinatal Psychosis, also known as "postpartum psychosis," is perhaps the most dangerous disorder for both the mother and the child. Most stories you hear about mothers that kill their infants (a.k.a. infanticide) or kill themselves, are situations where the mom was likely experiencing Perinatal Psychosis. Mothers will often keep quiet because they are embarrassed by their symptoms, or they are afraid their friends and family will think they are "crazy." Sometimes, these moms will open up about their symptoms, but family will not take them seriously or think that the mother is joking, stating things like, *"You just need to get some rest,"* or *"Don't be silly, you're just tired and anxious."* These kinds of comments, although intended to be helpful, are actually very invalidating. Moms will often

---

[4]Abramowitz, JS, et al. "Obsessive-compulsive symptoms in pregnancy and the puerperium: A review of the literature." *Journal of Anxiety Disorders*, vol. 17, no. 4, 2003, pp.461-478.

feel like no one understands them, and might isolate further from friends and family. This can lead to worsening of symptoms, and a potential emergency situation.

As I write this book, statistics show that Perinatal Psychosis is the leading cause of death for women the first year after their baby is born in Australia and England. Perinatal Psychosis is a *medical emergency* requiring *immediate treatment.* If you or someone you know is suffering from this disorder, pick up the phone and call a mental health professional immediately!

The following is a list of symptoms commonly associated with Perinatal Psychosis:

o Auditory Hallucinations (i.e. hearing noises, voices, or things that others do not hear)
o Visual Hallucinations (i.e. seeing figures, animals, bugs, creatures, or shadows that others do not see)
o Delusions
o Depressed Mood
o Desires or Thoughts of Harming the Baby
o Paranoia
o Irritable Mood or Agitation
o Suicidal Ideation
o Homicidal Ideation (usually of killing the baby)
o Sleep Problems (*Note: Remember, we are looking for an inability to sleep, even when the parent has the opportunity to do so!)
o Changes in Appetite (*Note: Again, either the parent does not eat at all or she eats all the time. It is the change we are looking for.)

The hallmark of this disorder is the delusions that accompany it. Although mothers with severe depression might also experience delusions, the delusions in Perinatal Psychosis are a little different. Typically, the delusions in this disorder have a "religious" or "spiritual" flavor to them, though not always. Mothers might talk about the baby "being possessed by a demon," or say that she "gave birth to the anti-Christ." In some occasions, the mom might say that "something is *wrong* with the baby." When she says this, she does not mean that she thinks the baby has a cold or the flu. She deeply believes that there is something *wrong* with it.

These delusions are different from the intrusive thoughts in Perinatal OCD because, in this case, the mom really believes them! She truly fears that the baby is somehow "wrong," "possessed," or "evil." Furthermore, she will have thoughts of killing or harming the baby because she is trying to save the baby's "soul" from the demon, or she is trying to protect the world from Satan himself! These thoughts and fears cause extreme distress for the mother, make her significantly anxious, depressed, and, oftentimes, lead to her harming the baby or infanticide. In fact, there is a 4% chance that a mother experiencing Perinatal Psychosis *will* kill her child[5]. Many women will become extremely suicidal when having Postpartum Psychosis because they are so depressed, or because they have harmed or killed their baby, leading to extreme emotional anguish and guilt.

---

[5] Friedman S.H. and Resnick, P.J. "Child murder by mothers: Patterns and prevention." *World Psychiatry,* vol. 6, no. 3, 2007, pp. 137-141.

Getting Help

In my opinion, the saddest part of maternal mental health disorders is that they are significantly under diagnosed and go largely untreated. Though our society is becoming more aware of these issues, there are still a large number of men and women who do not get the help that they need and deserve. That is why it is so important to be aware of these symptoms, to talk to your partner about what they are feeling, and to also be honest with yourself! If you feel like no one is listening to you, then become your own advocate and seek help from a therapist.

The good news is that, once diagnosed, maternal mental health disorders are very treatable. Treatment starts with establishing a good support network for mom and the baby. This might include enlisting friends, grandparents, siblings, and neighbors to help manage cooking, cleaning, and childcare. Sleep is particularly important, and one of the quickest ways to help mom (or dad) feel better. Uninterrupted sleep is essential to basic human functioning and development. Most parents will state that they are not a "good" parent if they do not get their rest. This is normal! So please, make time to sleep! If you can't sleep, then please see your doctor or request a referral for a Reproductive Psychiatrist who can prescribe medications that are compatible with being pregnant or breast-feeding.

Apart from sleep, proper nutrition and avoiding drugs and alcohol are important steps towards feeling better. Good nutrition helps to provide you with energy and can actually improve your mood. Avoiding drugs and alcohol can help keep you from feeling depressed, anxious, or paranoid, which in turn will reduce your stress. Another big help is seeking healthy stress-management activities that can help you relax, rest, and gain some quiet time.

Finally, call your health insurance company, or talk to your doctor about referrals to a mental health professional or clinic. It is amazing how much better you will feel when you get the opportunity to talk about your symptoms (or simply talk about how overwhelmed you feel) with someone you know you can trust and won't judge you! See if you can get connected with a Mommy Support Group too, where you can meet with other local moms struggling through some of the same issues. Whatever you choose to do, please seek help! There is no reason for your postpartum days to be miserable. You _can_ be happy! I promise! And you deserve it too!

12. FINDING HAPPINESS AMONGST THE STRESS

By now, you have come to realize that raising a baby or toddler is difficult work, regardless if you are a stay-at-home mom or if you are a working mom. You have also realized that having a baby is not all butterflies, smiles, giggles, and cuddles either. There is a lot of sweat, tears, and exhaustion that go into it too! It is definitely a mixed bag, and you never know if your bag has more smiles or tears in it! The important message that I want to convey in this text, however, is that you are not alone. There are thousands of other moms and dads who know exactly what you are going through, and they can relate in every way. Furthermore, there are many tips, ideas, and advice out there that can help make your journey through parenthood much easier.

We have come a long way at this point, discussing tips for choosing childcare, tips for running your household after work, discussed breast-feeding, and talked about basic discipline, among other topics. The last topic I want to chat with you about is self-care. Although the hundreds of baby books out there mention self-care, I feel that they do not really delve into it too much, and this is a disservice to you in my opinion. Yes, there is a baby that you need to care for, but you can't forget about <u>YOU</u> in the process either!

In my practice as a therapist, I have met people from all walks of life, all races, religions, ethnicities, and all socio-economic statuses. One of the greatest commonalities among most of my clients is the lack of self-care. Caring for everyone else, and failing to care for *yourself*, is a one-way ticket into my office; I can almost guarantee it! And new parents are at the top of that list! Does this mean you forget about your kids, or your spouse, or your dog and just focus solely on you? No… that is not it either. Rather, what I want to help you seek is a balance. Balance is a key to many things in life, and it is certainly a key here too.

As parents, we often place our children on the top of our "Care List," and then, we frequently will place our spouse, home, and work towards the top of that list too, with ourselves at the very bottom. At some point in Rachel's first year of life, I figured out that I did not even have myself on the Care List at all! Instead of sleeping, I would do dishes. Instead of showering, I would bathe Rachel. Instead of taking 5 minutes to rub some lotion on my dry hands, I would fold laundry. It took me yelling at my infant because she would not stop crying and getting so sick that I had to take two weeks off of work without pay before I realized that something was very wrong with this picture. I was lacking balance… and my

K.C. DREISBACH, LMFT

body and mind were giving up the fight.

Today, I recognize the importance of balance, of having time for my little girl and husband, but also for myself. I also recognize, however, how difficult it can be to find this balance when you are a parent. So, as with all the other important topics we have discussed, I met with other working moms and dads to find out their tips for managing and engaging in self-care.

Tip # 1: Please Sleep!

The most important tip, for so many different reasons, is to sleep. Sleep is just as important as drinking water in many ways. Your mind will completely fall apart if you do not let yourself sleep. I had a client who once suffered from chronic insomnia. She ended up developing psychosis (hearing and seeing things that are not really there) and becoming suicidal. Once her psychiatrist and I finally got her to sleep regular hours every night, all the depression and psychosis went away! Imagine that? A few nights of good rest and her depression was gone, like flipping a switch. As I said, sleep is very important. So please, treat this as a primary need, and get rest. I know this is a lot easier said than done. So, let us talk about ways to sneak in some sleep in your already busy schedule:

1. **Sleep when the Baby Sleeps**- Ok, I believe this is a lie because my baby never slept! But, if your little one *does* go down for regular naps, try to sleep when he does. I know you are tempted to do dishes, laundry, and make dinner, but remember, you will be a better parent if you get some sleep. So, pick only one of his naps to do

housework, and then take the other naps as your opportunity to get some rest.

2. **Ask a Friend, Relative, or Neighbor to Come Over and Babysit-** Your family and friends will be dying to come visit you and the baby. So, take this, and use it to your advantage. When my sister had her son, I would come over to visit, but she would often take the opportunity to shower and sleep while I watched her son. This is a great idea! And, if you can arrange Grandma to come Mondays, Auntie Mary to come Tuesdays, Uncle Fred to come Wednesdays, etc., then you can have a dedicated naptime for yourself every day of the week!

3. **Alternate Shifts with Your Partner-** At night, you know your baby is going to wake-up every few hours looking for food. Try alternating shifts with your partner so that you can both get rest. One couple I know would alternate by day. For example, Mom would take Monday, Wednesday, and Friday nights, while Dad would take on Tuesday, Thursday, and Sunday nights. They would both share Saturday nights.

    o Another option for alternating shifts might be splitting the night in half. If Dad goes to bed normally around ten o'clock p.m., then he can watch the baby until two in the morning while Mom sleeps. Then, Mom can take over from two until the baby decides she is up for the day.

    o Another way to alternate shifts is to have

one parent tend the baby every other time. For example, when the baby gets up at eleven o'clock in the evening, Mom can do it. When the baby gets up again at two in the morning, it will be Dad's turn. Then, at five o'clock in the morning, Mom will take over again, etc.

I am sure you can think of other ways to alternate shifts, so try them! Do not be afraid to try different methods until you find something that works for you.

4. **Go to Bed Early-** I was never an "early to bed" kind of person, but that really changed once I had Rachel. As you already know at this point, Rachel was a terrible sleeper, and I found myself always desperate for sleep. I finally decided that if Rachel was going to go down for bed at eight o'clock in the evening, I was going to call it a night too because I knew she would be up in a few hours. Thus, my "early to bed" days began, and it really did help. Although I hated coming home from work, making dinner, eating, getting her ready for bed, and then going to bed myself without ever getting a chance to unwind, the extra sleep was very important! Having those extra hours helped me to keep my cool when it was 3:00 a.m. and Rachel decided it was time to play. Remember, too, that this is only for a little while. Eventually, she began sleeping through the night (well, almost...), and then I was able to afford staying up later after she fell asleep. So, rest now and know that you will be able to enjoy drinks

after the baby's asleep in the future.

5. **Take a Night Off-** In the beginning, my parents were always offering to take Rachel for me at night, but I always turned them down. I was terrified at the thought of not having her with me, and I would miss her so much that I never took advantage of the offers. As my fears subsided, however, I was more willing to let Rachel spend the night with her grandparents, and this was a blessing. Although I did not *want* her to spend the night with her grandparents, I *needed* her to so that I could get some solid, uninterrupted rest. Getting those nights to recharge my batteries was essential and important. If you can find someone you trust to take your baby or toddler for the night once a week, I highly recommend it! If once a week is too often for you, try once every other week, or perhaps once a month. It is amazing what a night or two of good, solid sleep does for a sleep- deprived parent.

Tip # 2: Be Sure to Take a Bath or Shower

Showering, or taking a bath, is very relaxing. Washing the day's worries and troubles down the drain can have a very soothing effect on your psyche. Unfortunately, many people will forego the shower for the sake of time. (I am hugely guilty of this!) Please, take a bath! Good self-care starts with the essentials, and showering or bathing are definitely part of that. Shower, shave, wash your hair, etc. Find a shower gel that has a scent you love and use that to lather up.

If you want to get super fancy, and have the budget

for it, buy some essential oils and use an oil diffuser to make your bathroom smell heavenly. Essential oils have therapeutic properties and have been shown to have wonderful health benefits. Look online for different scents and the health benefits they have to offer you. Then, use the essential oil that corresponds to your need. For example, essential oils frequently used for stress are lavender, sandalwood, jasmine, neroli, orange, and lemon balm. Buy one you like, put a few drops in a diffuser (follow the directions to the diffuser) and enjoy!

Another way to help yourself with your self-care is to pamper yourself a little bit. Get a massage, get your nails done, or get a facial. I know these things can be expensive, but who says you have to go out to a salon to get them done? Enlist your spouse to give you a quick rub with a lotion you really enjoy. Paint your own nails while listening to soothing music, or ask your sister or a girlfriend if they wouldn't mind helping you out with a pedicure at home! Don't have enough time? Why not make a sugar scrub that you can use in the shower to exfoliate your skin? There are hundreds of "do it yourself" recipes on how to make sugar scrubs, and they are incredibly easy to do. One of my favorites is one I created on my very own. I make it for friends and family from time to time, and they all love it. Here it is:

DIY Cucumber Sugar Scrub
½ cup coconut oil
½ cup pureed cucumber
3 cups refined white sugar
A squeeze of fresh lemon juice (optional)

1.   Mix all of the ingredients in a bowl until well

combined.

2. Spoon the mixture into an air-tight container, such as a mason jar, & enjoy!
3. Store it in the refrigerator to keep it fresh longer.

Tip # 3: Eat Nutritiously

Ok, we all know "you are what you eat!" Eating a healthy diet can help us feel better, look better, have more energy, and reduce stress. Get in those fruits and veggies, cut down on the sugar and carbs, and drink alcohol and caffeine (if any) in moderation. Check with your doctor to make sure that you are not deficient in any vitamins, such as Vitamin D, and if you are, follow through with your doctor's recommendations.

As a working parent, it is really too easy to rely on fast food, canned goods, or frozen TV dinners for quick, easy meals. But this really is not the best for you or your baby. Try to buy fresh or frozen fruits and vegetables, and use the tips listed in the previous chapters to help you make nutritious meals that are good for you and your family.

One co-worker of mine is a single mom with two boys, and she has a hard time eating her veggies because she does not like the taste. To solve this problem, she "juices." She brings a blender to work and will blend all kinds of veggies and fruits together to make smoothies or juices filled with healthy veggies for lunch! This is also a great trick to get your kids to eat more veggies too! After all, what kid doesn't like smoothies? Start off with more fruits to make the juice sweeter. Then, slowly reduce the fruit and increase the veggies to wean your taste buds off the sweetness of the fruit and up your vegetable count. Try this same trick with your kids to help them grow to like the veggie taste. Also, toddlers have a way of turning their nose up at "new" or suspicious-looking foods. If you have a kid like this, try putting the drink in a tumbler cup with a straw (one that is not clear). If they can't see what they are drinking, they are less likely to turn their nose up at it.

Tip #4: Do Not Skip Meals

Skipping meals is not a great idea, especially if you need a good source of energy all day long. As mentioned, food gives you energy, and if you are going to keep up with your toddler or baby, you will need all the energy you can get! I remember when Rachel was really little, there were many times when I would totally forget to eat! I would be so busy with cleaning the house, doing my homework, and caring for her that I would completely lose my appetite and skip meals. Not a great idea, *especially* if you are pumping or breastfeeding!

To avoid this big no-no, try to snack or eat something whenever your baby eats. This serves as a great reminder to eat (after all, your baby will not forget *he's* hungry), and you will get the opportunity to model nutritious eating habits for your child. Plus, eating together is a great, social bonding experience for children. If you remember earlier in this text, I talk about the psychological benefits that sharing family meals can have on children. So eat up! Even if all you can eat is an apple, a meal replacement shake, or a granola bar... eat something! And if all else fails, take a multivitamin. It is not nearly as good as consuming the right foods, but it is better than nothing.

Tip #5: Get Out of the House!

New moms often feel very housebound. They worry so much about the baby getting sick, or feel so overwhelmed about taking all the baby gear with them to the store that they would rather just stay at home. One mom I spoke to would never leave the house unless someone went with her! Can you imagine seeing the same four walls every day with no one to talk to except the non-verbal child? Not a great idea, and a great way to induce depression, anxiety, or some other mental health conditions.

Please, get out of your home! I do not care if all you do is take a walk around the block, but get out of your house! A great idea my sister gave me was having two diaper bags. One was a giant monster-of-a-thing that fit anything and everything under the sun! It had clothes, formula, bottled water, toys, dried snacks (such as individually packaged crackers), diapers, wipes, bottles, pacifier, blankets, probably a kitchen sink, etc. She always left this one in the car. Then, she would have a little bag that looked like an over-sized purse. In here, she kept the bare essentials: 1 bottle (already filled with water to make formula), 1 pacifier, 1 bib, formula, 1 snack, a few diapers, a few wipes, her wallet, her cell phone, and her car keys. That is it. When she would go to the store, she would grab this little bag and take off. She would not worry about checking the bag or packing anything up. Just grab and go. If she was in the store and realized she was out of wipes, she would just go to the car and grab the giant diaper bag to restock. Why did this help? Because if she decided to leave the house, she did not have to spend 2 hours packing the diaper bag and car with baby stuff. It was already done. Just remember to check the bag and restock every week, if needed.

I hated packing a stroller wherever I went. It was so cumbersome, and Rachel would cry half the time in it anyways. My big secret to sanity was having a Moby Wrap. I would wrap it on my body before I left the house, and when I got to the store, I would slip Rachel in it, put a diaper, small package of wipes, and her bottle in my purse and hit the road! Baby-wearing was a *must* for me! Rachel was happy and would usually sleep, and I got to use my arms and go about my daily duties. It made taking Rachel out by myself a much easier task that did not seem nearly so daunting.

Tip #6: Socialize

It is not good enough to just get out of the house; You have to meet and talk with other adults! Even individuals who run daycare facilities have contact with other adults all day long, so of course you need it too! Children are a blessing, and I am one of the first people you will find saying this, but children do not stimulate adult minds. As such, if you stay home with your baby all day, every day, you might find yourself getting a little cabin fever. This is where Mom's Groups or Parenting Support groups come in.

In my private practice, I offered Parenting Support services to moms and dads who felt they needed a little extra help managing their child, but I also had parents who came in looking for a little "me time." They wanted to know that, at least one hour a week, they could focus on themselves, talk to someone, complain, cry, laugh, or simply sit in silence. I remember my sister joined a Mom's Group when her son was born, and to this day, those moms still get together with their little ones to socialize. I have another girlfriend who joined an online community of moms. They would set up chat times in the evening where they would all go online and chat with one another about different trials and tribulations of parenthood.

The point is that, it really does not matter how you do it, as long as you do it! Online, in person, or paid for, just meet up with other people and talk with one another! Research has shown that human beings require socialization and have a deep, inner desire to feel like they *belong*. You will find that regularly getting together with other adults will greatly help reduce your cabin fever, and it will act as a protective factor against some of those maternal mental health issues we discussed previously.

Tip #7: Get Some Physical Exercise

Ugh! Did I just mention exercise? Yes... yes I did. As you probably already know, exercise is an important piece of the puzzle when it comes to good self-care. Not only does exercise actually release endorphins, which are chemicals in your body that reduce your body's perception of pain, but research has now shown that people who are physically fit are less likely to suffer from depression! Furthermore, if you already suffer from depression or anxiety, exercise can help reduce your symptoms. The reason why is because those endorphins that decrease the sensation of pain also make you feel emotionally happy! That is a win-win situation right there in my book!

Now, you might be thinking that you are going to have to get a membership to the gym, but not necessarily.

Exercise does not have to be jogging on a treadmill or lifting weights. Exercise can also consist of taking a walk, swimming, yoga, or aerobics, among others. The big question I get, however, is how do I fit in exercise when I already have everything else on my To Do list? That is a great question, and it honestly comes down to getting creative. For example, you might consider going for a walk around the block with your baby in tow! If you push your child in a stroller, you will get a better work out, too, than if you just went for a walk on your own. If you are me, however, your baby may not be too keen on the stroller. I remember Rachel would cry every time I tried putting her in the stroller. So what did I do? I started wearing her of course! Remember that Moby Wrap I talked about earlier? I would wrap her up in that and hit the road!

Another idea might be to include your toddler in the exercise routine. If you have a toddler who can follow basic directions, he might get a kick out of playing Simon Says "Exercise!" You be Simon and instruct your Little One to stretch, do jumping jacks, try crunches, run around the sofa, lunges, etc. My guess is, he will be laughing the whole time, while you get in a few minutes of endorphin-releasing movements! And, by the way, you are also sneaking in some quality time. You get some exercise in combination with playtime. Now *that* is killing two birds with one stone!

Now, what if you have a baby? You might be able to have the baby lie down on a play mat or have tummy time while you follow an exercise routine nearby. If your baby is like my Rachel, however, she will cry up a storm. So how do you get that exercise in while carrying a baby?

(Drum roll please....) You wear the baby of course! Moby Wraps come with an instruction booklet that have exercises you can do while wearing your baby in a Moby Wrap. Imagine that! Other baby carriers might offer their own exercises you can do too, so look into it or research it online. The important, take home message is that you can find some time to exercise, even if you are a single parent with a toddler or baby.

Two final notes on exercise should be mentioned before moving on:

1. Do not over do it! That busy schedule and mile-long To Do List are a real thing, and you do not want yourself feeling additional pressure or stress trying to manage it all. Instead of trying to block big chunks of time to do an exercise routine, you might try finding some small clumps of time throughout your week. Research shows that the frequency in which you exercise is much more important than duration. This means that it is better for you, all around, if you exercise consistently a few times a week for a short time verses exercising every once in a while for hours. Try to set aside just 15 to 20 minutes a couple of times of week (3 – 4 times perhaps) instead of a 1-2 hour block of time once a week.

2. Make sure you talk to your doctor before starting anything. Some folks have physical limitations, making it difficult for them to do certain exercises. This would include women who recently delivered a baby, either vaginally or through cesarean procedure. Your doctor will be

153

able to help identify the best exercises for you given your current physical condition and any other physical limitations.

Tip #8: Stay Hydrated

This one seems pretty obvious, but many women do not get enough water during, or after, pregnancy! Hydration is very important to good self-care, and it is necessary if you are pumping or breastfeeding. Make sure you drink the recommended number of ounces, and remember that the recommendation changes if you are exercising, expressing milk or nursing. If you are not sure how much water you should be consuming, you can always speak to your doctor or try looking it up online.

Now, I know drinking water has never been one of my favorite tasks… mostly because I do not like the taste of water. While I was nursing, my lactation consultant reminded me that drinking water was essential to good milk production, and her recommendation was that I drink 1-2 glasses (that is 8 oz. per glass) of fluid (water preferably) whenever I breastfed Rachel. *Yuck!* I thought to myself, *How am I ever going to drink that much water?!?*

My lifesaver became flavored water. Not only can you buy water that is pre-flavored and enriched with vitamins (remember, ask your doctor if these are a good choice if you are pregnant or giving your child breastmilk), but you can also use stuff like Crystal Light that are low-calorie and come in a huge variety of flavors! I used to make a big pitcher of flavored water and chug away. Many stores make generic versions of Crystal Light too, which are a little cheaper and taste very similar.

This trick is also great for toddlers and kids who tend to prefer fruit juices over water. As your pediatrician might have already told you, juicing it up all the time is not great for their teeth and can make a child more prone to obesity. Remember, their growing bodies also need to stay hydrated too, so using flavored water for them is also a great idea. You can find a flavoring agent that tastes like fruit punch, which will satisfy their craving for that sweet taste while also minimizing their sugar consumption and increase their water intake.

Tip # 9: Enjoy a Hobby Whenever Possible

Most of us had something we enjoyed doing before we had kids. Some of us are artists, others knit or crochet, or maybe you were a runner. Some of us were into crafts and some of us into movies or fashion. The point is, we all did something for fun before we had kids, right? Even if all you did was read before bed, it was still something!

If you are like most mothers (or fathers!), you probably stopped engaging in these enjoyable activities once your little one was born. Am I right? Just could not find time anymore to knit that new scarf or read that next best seller. This is yet another example of how we place ourselves at the bottom of that Care List once we became parents. The sad part is that, engaging in hobbies or activities we find enjoyable is a huge protective factor against stress, anger/aggression, and depression! So, this tip is all about re-engaging yourself in something you love doing!

I have always been a bookworm. Reading before bed was one of my favorite activities. When I had

Rachel, I felt like I never had time to read anymore, and if I did manage to find time, I was always so tired that I never had enough energy to pick up the book! It took some time for me to finally come up with a creative way to incorporate reading into my life again, but once I did, I found that the long hours nursing were not really so bad.

I have mentioned that I nursed Rachel, but I do not think I really emphasized just *how much* I nursed her. Even though I only breastfed for 4 months, I was breastfeeding all the time! Rachel would nurse for 30 to 45 minutes *each breast!* That is one hour to 1 ½ hours each time! And then, she grew so fast those first 2 months that she would eat every 2 to 3 hours! That means that on a good day, I was breastfeeding for 8 hours of the day! The result was that I was very bored of breastfeeding, and I always felt she wanted to eat when it was the least opportune time. So, I tried doing different things while she fed. Mainly, I tried to read, but maneuvering her, the book, and the pillows I had to support her weight, was just such a pain. I gave up.

The best gift I ever got right before I had Rachel was given to me by my mother-in-law, and it was a Kindle. I was never into electronic reading devices (e-readers), and though I liked the gift, I just never used it. I remember complaining to my husband one night about having to breastfeed all the time and how bored I was feeling. That is when he mentioned using my Kindle to read. It was like a light bulb when off in my head and angels from heaven came out to sing! And then, I felt really stupid for not thinking of that first. Needless to say, I tried it, it worked, and breastfeeding was instantly much more enjoyable to me!

So, let's go back to our tip of engaging in hobbies. What is the point of this story about my breastfeeding woes? Well, the point is that you should try your best to keep up on your hobbies, if possible. And if you do not think it is possible, try brainstorming with a friend or your partner on ways you can incorporate a hobby into tasks you already do for your family. For me, it was reading while breastfeeding. For other moms or dads, it might be knitting while you watch Mickey Mouse Club House for the 10th time in a row, or encouraging your little artist to practice with crayons or experiment with non-toxic paint while you sketch a new masterpiece right next to them. Like so many other topics we have discussed, re-engaging in your hobby is about thinking of creative solutions, not getting stuck on the problem or what does not work. Try, try, and try again until you find something that works for you and baby too!

13. GOOD LUCK!

As I type this final chapter, Rachel is three years old. We have overcome the Terrible Two's, conquered potty training, and already beginning the next exciting (and totally terrifying) chapter of our lives, Baby Number 2! I think back to the sleepless nights, the non-stop tears (both hers and mine!), the breastfeeding struggles, juggling home and work, and the awful emotional tussles of the Baby Blues and guilt, and all I can say to you is good luck! Good luck, my friends, and hang in there because I promise you it gets better. It may not feel like it at times, and I know there are nights where you will swear that things are only getting worse. But it _will_ get better. Raising a child will always be a challenge, especially when you are a fulltime parent and are trying to manage a career on the side, but life has a funny way of working out for the better.

Raising Rachel has been one of the biggest challenges

of my life, and I know it will continue to be one of the biggest challenges in the future. But it has also been one of the greatest joys that I have ever experienced, and I cannot even dream of my life without her.

Remember to always take the journey one step at a time, and do not get so discouraged with the setbacks. No matter how hard or how difficult the journey appears, try to enjoy it as much as you can. Your Little One is only "little" for a little bit, and then they grow up. The opportunity to raise your child only occurs once in a lifetime (after all, you might have other children, but you only get to raise each child once), so try to hang on to every part of it, even the tough moments. Remember that raising your child is not a race, and you can take as long as you need to "get it right." And, if you have made some mistakes along the way, tomorrow is a new day, and you can always opt to make a better choice.

More importantly, remember to love your child every day, and tell them you care. Tell him he is handsome and smart, and that she is beautiful and intelligent. Tell them you love them… hug them, kiss them, and let them know that they will always be perfect in your eyes. No matter how old they get, they will always be your baby, and you will always be Mommy or Daddy. That child is yours forever, and you are theirs!

Remember to take care of yourself in this journey too, and to be gentle on yourself. After all, children do not come with an instruction manual, so you are bound to make some mistakes! Just remember to learn from them, seek help when you need it, and be open to suggestions and advice from those you trust or admire.

Be sure you engage in good self-care and do your best, because that is all anyone will expect from you.

Finally, remember that just because you have a baby or a toddler, it does not mean you need to throw all things you enjoy doing out the window! Having a baby or a toddler simply means you might need to make some adjustments and get a little creative.

I hope this book has given you some hope and faith in your own abilities to manage parenthood and find the balance you need in your life. If you find yourself needing some extra help, do not feel bad asking for it! There are thousands of qualified therapists who are willing to help support and guide you through the struggles. All you have to do is accept their assistance. So, as I mentioned before, good luck on your journey, and may it be restful, peaceful, and full of love and joy!

AUTHOR NOTE

Trials of the Working Parent was a lot of fun to write. I enjoyed reaching out to other moms and learning their secrets for making life work for them on a day-to-day basis. The experience was cathartic, in many ways, and it allowed me to feel validated as a parent myself, struggling to manage it all. That was my goal with *Trials*.... I wanted other parents to feel a sense of kinship, a sense of belonging, and to no longer feel alone. I hope you got that from reading this book.

For authors, book reviews are the lifeline! Without reviews, books disappear into oblivion and new readers can't find them. If you found this book to be even a *little* helpful to you on your parenting journey, please consider leaving an honest review on Amazon, Barnes & Noble, GoodReads, etc. It would mean so much to me!

Also, I absolutely love talking to readers. Consider reaching out to me on my website if you have any parenting questions or simply want to chat or have a parenting story you would like to share. I have a parenting blog that I update regularly, and I send out monthly emails with parenting quotes I love and updates on what's going on in my life. You can subscribe at www.kcdreisbach.com.

Finally, you can also find me on Facebook @kcdreisbach. It's a great place to connect with other parents facing your same struggles! I post helpful parenting articles, inspirational quotes, and fun parenting memes. Come check it out!

Enjoy other books by K.C. Dreisbach and continue to help your family grow in love and unity:

Eliminating Temper Tantrums: 4 Keys to Mastering Your Child's Anger Outbursts

ACKNOWLEDGMENTS

Some believe that a great book writes itself. While I think that this may be true, to some extent, it is not entirely true. Every great book has many people who take a part in its creation. From the source of inspiration, to the individual who provides the gritty details, many people are involved in the birth of a new book. Although a great book may write itself, it does not create itself. As such, there are several people who I want to acknowledge for their part in making this book a reality.

My father and mother truly deserve the largest amount of acknowledgment because their dedication to being parents before anything else is tremendously admirable. I love you both very much, and I thank you for always encouraging me to do my best, to always have hope, and to never give up!

I also want to give a giant thank you to my husband for his never-ending support of my dreams. Although skeptical at times, his realism and logical ways of thinking always kept me grounded, no matter how "fantastical" my ideas or plans became. When the time came to take a leap of faith into publishing this book, he was there, cheering me on.

To my "Tina," who was a second mother to me. Her strength, love, and patience knew no bounds, and she tirelessly pushed to motivate me to succeed... mostly so I wouldn't get into trouble. I promised her that, one day, I would write and publish a book, and that she would be one of the first to get an "autographed copy." I will keep my promise.

Now, when we talk about creation of a book, the editor certainly plays a major role. For that, my sister deserves a large thank you! She did me the favor and read this book over tirelessly, looking for the slightest typo or grammatical imperfection to improve your reading enjoyment. Thank you, Kassandra, for your time, energy, and effort in playing this most vital role!

And finally, I wish to acknowledge Rick and Maggie Hunt, who have been a part of my life since childhood. They always encouraged me to write as much as my heart desired, and they calmed my parents' fears about my future success. They knew I would write and publish one day before I even dreamed it a reality. I will always appreciate your faith in me. Thank you.

BIBLIOGRAPHY

Abramowitz, JS, et al. "Obsessive-compulsive symptoms in pregnancy and the puerperium: A review of the literature." *Journal of Anxiety Disorders*, vol. 17, no. 4, 2003, pp.461-478.

"American Academy of Pediatrics Announces New Safe Sleep Recommendations to Protect Against SIDS, Sleep-Related Infant Deaths." *American Academy of Pediatrics*, American Academy of Pediatrics, 2016, www.aap.org/en-us/about-the-aap/aap-press-room/pages/american-academy-of-pediatrics-announces-new-safe-sleep-recommendations-to-protect-against-sids.aspx, Accessed 13 April 2017.

Blair, P.S., Fleming, D., Bensley, et. al. Where Should Babies Sleep – Along or With Parents? Factors Influencing the Risk Of SIDS in the CESDI Study." *British Medical Jounral,* vol. 319, 1999, pp.1457-1462.

"Childhood Anxiety Disorders." *Anxiety and Depression Association of America*, Sept. 2015, https://www.adaa.org/livingwithanxiety/children/childhood-anxiety-disorders. Accessed 19 April 2017.

Friedman S.H. and Resnick, P.J. "Child murder by mothers: Patterns and prevention." *World Psychiatry,* vol. 6, no. 3, 2007, pp. 137-141.

Heron, P. "Non-Reactive Cosleeping and Child Behavior: Getting a Good Night's Sleep All Night, Every Night." Master's thesis, Department of Psychology, University of Bristol, 1994.

Holly, Homer, and Miller, Rachel. *101 Kids Activities That*

Are the Bestest, Funnest Ever!: The Entertainment Solution for Parents, Relatives & Babysitters!. Page Street Publishing, 2014.

Holly, Homer, et al. *The 101 Coolest Science Experiments: Awesome Thing To Do With Your Parents, Babysitters and Other Adults*. Page Street Publishing, 2016.

"Pregnancy & Postpartum Mental Health: Perinatal Mood & Anxiety Disorders Overview." *Postpartum Support International*, www.postpartum.net/learn-more/pregnancy-postpartum-mental-health/. Accessed 13 April 2017.

"Teen Brain: Behavior, Problem Solving, and Decision Making." *American Academy of Child & Adolescent Psychiatry*, no. 95, American Academy of Child & Adolescent Psychiatry, 2016, www.aacap.org/AACAP/Families_and_Youth/Facts_for_Families/FFF-Guide/The-Teen-Brain-Behavior-Problem-Solving-and-Decision-Making-095.aspx, Accessed 13 April 2017.

"Benefits of Family Dinners." *The Family Dinner Project*, www.thefamilydinnerproject.org/about-us/benefits-of-family-dinners/. Accessed 13 April 2017.

"How else does the Affordable Care Act impact breastfeeding families?." *The United States Breastfeeding Committee*, www.usbreastfeeding.org/p/cm/ld/fid=249. Accessed 13 April 2017.

"Workplace Support in Federal Law: What is the "Break Time for Nursing Mothers" law?." *The United States Breastfeeding Committee*, www.usbreastfeeding.org/p/cm/ld/fid=200. Accessed 13 April 2017.

Zambaldi, CF, et al. "Postpartum obsessive-compulsive disorder: Prevalence and clinical characteristics."

Comprehensive Psychiatry, vol. 50, no. 6, 2009, pp. 503-509.

ABOUT THE AUTHOR

K.C. Dreisbach is a licensed Marriage & Family Therapist in Southern California. She graduated from Loma Linda University with her Master's of Science in Marital & Family Therapy, and has been practicing in the Mental Health field ever since. She has spent the last 7 years working with troubled teens, and has a passion for helping struggling parents manage home, work, and family life. In her spare time, she enjoys reading, horseback riding, writing works of fiction, and spending time with her husband and two young children.

Made in the USA
Coppell, TX
20 March 2020

17200641R00104